JUST ADD
BEER

Bringing beer, food and
Cornwall together with over
60 inspiring recipes

JUST ADD
BEER

ED HUGHES AND
RACHEL WILLIAMS

Editor Louise Searle
Copy Editor Hayley Spurway
Photographer Guy Harrop
Designer Colin Berwick
Proof Reader Cai Waggett

Contributing Photographers
Toby Lowe p26

Printed by Deltor Printing, Cornwall
Published by Muse Media
Distributed by Salt Media

Just Add Beer ISBN 978-1-9996478-0-3

The view from The Mariners, looking out over the beautiful Camel Estuary.

CONTENTS

FOREWORD

Throughout history, beer has always been a popular beverage. It's even believed that in medieval Europe more people consumed beer because the brewing process made it safer than water. However, it's not until recently that beer has been matched with food. Traditionally, foodies have matched dishes with wine. But that's all about to change. A new era is emerging, in which people are discovering that beer can be a wonderful accompaniment to food, and that there are lots of different brews to suit all palates.

Through my relationship with Sharp's Brewery, I've come to understand the different aspects and subtle flavours of beer. Matching them with dishes at my restaurants has been fun, and something of a revelation. It's amazing how a certain beer can complement the individual flavours in a dish, enhancing the overall enjoyment of a meal.

Of course, people have been cooking with beer for a while: beer battered fish is quite commonplace and stout is often added to rich beef stews. So why stop there? We also use beer in bread, for curing foods and even in some desserts.

In this cookery book, Sharp's Brewery has collected an array of recipes from prominent chefs working with the wonderful produce we have in Cornwall. Embracing the idea of food being paired with beers, these chefs have been experimenting in their kitchens to create these recipes, using beer, for you to try. I'm sure you'll be delighted with the results. So, bottoms up, cook and enjoy!

NATHAN OUTLAW
Seafood chef and author

INTRODUCTION

ED HUGHES - BEER SOMMELIER, SHARP'S BREWERY

Why is it that so many people know a Rioja from a Riesling, yet hardly anyone knows the difference between ale and lager? And while many of us pair Syrah and steak, or seafood and Sauvignon, when we talk about food and beer it's usually limited to a pie and pint of ale, or a curry and a cooling lager.

As a foodie and beer sommelier working with Sharp's Brewery and some of the finest chefs with their roots in Cornwall, it's become my mission to educate and inspire people about

the modern, mouth-watering fusion of beer and food. Beer shouldn't be an afterthought. It should be at the heart of any dining experience. So the aim of this book is to turn the pint drinking culture on its head, put beer on its rightful pedestal and have you swapping your Pinot for a Pilsner at the dinner table.

My own beer epiphany happened early in my hospitality career, over a beautiful chalice of Leffe Blonde in Belgium. Before then I'd known grape varieties and wines, and I'd known spirits and cocktails; but all I knew about beer was pubs and pints. Yet when I experienced the respect and reverence given to beer in Brussels, I looked at beer in a completely different light.

It was working with the incredible Nathan Outlaw that first sparked my interest about how chefs consider ingredients, and how beer and food could work together. I also gleaned inspiration from Tristan Stephenson's encyclopaedic knowledge about spirits and history, and from my beer hero Stuart Howe – former Head Brewer at Sharp's. And so my beer and food journey began. Since then I've been committed to working with chefs, front of house teams and the general public, to raise the profile of beer and promote it as a food match equal to wine.

A collaboration between Sharp's Brewery and a pool of talented chefs, our book celebrates bringing friends and family together for sociable occasions, and puts beer on the table alongside easy-to-make, lip-smacking recipes. Beer is thousands of years old and we truly believe that there is a beer for every palate, every dish and every occasion – whether you want to throw a fancy dinner party or kick back and watch a sports game with friends. In the same way that photos evoke memories of special occasions, so do certain foods and flavours. Marrying the right food with the right beer, and putting it in the mix with friends and family at birthdays, BBQs and festive occasions, creates unforgettable experiences that spike our senses.

The first time that the team at Sharp's brought the concept of food and beer matching to the public was through our Secret Bar, at a festival in Ireland. Dressed in a velvet jacket, I served beer and food in a deer shed decked out with chandeliers and old dining tables. The juxtaposition of the muddy festival and beer swigging culture against this more refined ambience, was all part of our plan to disrupt the senses and alter people's perceptions of beer. After that we launched the bar in a shipping container at the Padstow Christmas Festival, where a secret door led into a plush speakeasy bar where beer was matched with food from some of the region's finest chefs. From here our relationship with the chefs of Padstow and beyond mushroomed, and every chef featured

in this book has been part of the Secret Bar and our beer and food journey. I'm humbled to have worked with such wonderful and talented people, and this book wouldn't exist without their support and contributions.

Now that the general public are more savvy about flavour and quality than they ever have been, it's time to make beer and food matching part of the future of gastronomy. So, gather your friends and family, get creative in the kitchen and discover the dynamic delights of food and beer.

HOW TO PAIR BEER & FOOD

DISCOVER THE RIGHT BEER FOR EVERY DISH

*Sweet, bitter, sour, spicy and fruity:
Beer arguably has even more complex
tasting notes and flavours than wine
and we believe that there is a beer to
suit every palate and every dish.*

Beer and food matching is a growing concept in
modern cuisine, so there are no hard and fast rules.
It's best to experiment with different beers and
flavours, and not to feel constrained by anything
other than what tastes great together. As a
general guide, think about beer and food pairing
just like wine and food. For example, if you'd serve
a crisp white wine with a certain dish, swap it for
a refreshing, light lager. For meals that go best
with full-bodied reds, try amber or dark beers to
balance the more robust flavours. And remember
that each palate is different, so what works for one
person might not work for another.

To get you started on your own voyage of discovery,
follow our introductory guide:

THE FOUR CS

Cleanse
To refresh the palate, choose a highly carbonated
lager, such as a Helles-style lager or a bottled Pale Ale.

Cut
Cut through rich creamy sauces with the intense
bitterness of a hop forward New World IPA or a
Double IPA.

Complement
Try to match the ingredients of the dish with
ingredients that have been used in the brewing
process. For example, if there is fennel in the dish
try a beer that has used fennel in the brewing
process, such as Sharp's Chalky's Bite.

Contrast

Sometimes there is no rhyme or reason why beer and food matches work, they just do. One style of beer can have so many variances and match many different types of food. So this is your chance to try something new and put contrasting flavours together. It can be risky, but it's great when it works.

To work out what sorts of foods beer might match with, take into consideration a few of the qualities of the beer:

BODY

Does your dish lend itself to a light, dry beer, or a full-bodied bitter? Generally, beer with a full body will work better with richer foods, such as creamy dishes or cheese. A delicate, crisp beer tends to go better with lighter dishes, yet it can also counterbalance fatty or salty foods.

BUBBLES

Carbonated beer is refreshing and can lift the richness of heavy dishes. However, watch out for very fizzy beers when you're eating spicy foods, because bubbles can accentuate the heat of the chilli.

BITTERNESS

Bitter beers can be as refreshing as bubbly beers, especially when paired with salt and fat. Bitterness can also balance out sweet foods; for example, try Stout with chocolate, or an IPA with cake.

SWEETNESS

Those lovely malty, sweet tones in beers match with many different foods, but are especially good with spicy, sweet and rich foods.

ACIDITY

It's really only the Lambic and Sour Ales that boast the acidity akin to wines. Try them with salty and fatty dishes.

TEMPERATURE

Traditionalists might suggest that ales should be served at room temperature, while lagers should be served fridge-cold. But we're not traditionalists. So we suggest that you experiment with drinking beers at different temperatures. However, if a beer is served too cold it will dull the aromas and flavours; if a beer is too warm, it will accentuate some of the lesser-desired flavours. Try to drink beers no lower than 4°C and no higher than 13°C. A cold lager pairs beautifully with fresh seafood on a summer's day, yet equally, an Amber Ale served at cellar temperature (12-13°C) makes the perfect partner to a Cornish crab sandwich.

USING BEER AS AN INGREDIENT

Beer is an excellent ingredient to add to a huge variety of dishes. Not only because adding a dash of beer to your recipe means that you can enjoy cooking with a delicious beer in hand. You can substitute beer for water, wine, stock – any liquid ingredients – to add a twist to your dish, and also use it for brining, basting, braising and dressing.

TOP FOOD PAIRING TIPS

1 Treat beer like wine. Swill it, smell it, sip it. Respect it

2 Be inquisitive. If you're in a restaurant or pub, ask the staff to recommend new beer and food matches.

3 Match lighter beers with lighter flavours and darker beers with fuller flavours.

4 As well as matching your beer with food, use beer as an ingredient in your cooking for a more advanced integration of flavour. (See the 'Beeramisu' recipe on page 132).

5 Take the time to try the different flavours for yourself. From there the ideas will usually click. Theoretical matches don't always work, so it's a great excuse to buy a selection of beers and find out what works for your tastes.

Try Porthilly and Doom Bar Mussels on p72

To get you started with pairing beer and food, we've suggested a beer to match every recipe in this book. Each chapter is based around an occasion, from everyday classics and beer snacks, to celebration dishes and hearty roasts. Here are a few basic matches to get your taste buds tingling:

AL FRESCO

Hot dogs, tacos and sensational salads - it's all about taking tasty food outdoors and making the most of sunny days. When the weather's good it's easy to turn to an ice-cold lager for refreshment, but how about trying a Pale Ale to reinforce the fresh, seasonal flavours of the Asparagus Salad on page 50.

EVERYDAY MEALS

Even if you're short on time on a weeknight, it doesn't mean you can't serve up a delicious dish such as crab tagliatelle or pizza, alongside a light, refreshing Pilsner or Pale Ale.

COCKTAILS AND CANAPÉS

Did you know that beer is an excellent ingredient for cocktails? Try a Peach Smash with Sharp's Sea Fury (page 79) and you'll see what we mean.

BEER SNACKS

When you're watching a match with mates, serve up classic snacks such as pork crackling and chilli nuts, alongside something like a Czech Pilsner to balance the salty, spicy flavours.

ROASTS

The Sunday roast is something of an institution in British culture, and tastes even better after a windswept coastal walk. Beers with smoky and malty tones pair well with the rich meats and sauces. Try matching a Best Bitter with Steve Marsh's Roast Beef on page 116.

CELEBRATIONS

We love an excuse to make cake, and expert patisserie chef Stuart Pate has nailed the art of pairing sweet foods with beer. Why not try his incredible Chocolate Pyramid Cake on page 154 with a rich Porter or Stout?

WINTER WARMERS

Think curries, stews and pies - the sort of dishes we crave after a winter's day in the great outdoors. Whether you've been for a dip in the surf or a stroll along the coast path, warm up with an IPA and a Beef and Smoked Potato Pie (page 162).

LARDER AND CHEESE

Pairing cheese and beer is perhaps the simplest way to start beer and food matching at home. There is no cooking required, the options are almost endless and beer is an excellent accompaniment to cheese, cutting through the fat. So prepare a Doom Bar Pear Chutney (page 177) and swap your bottle of Port for a Porter next time the cheeseboard comes out.

 "There is a type of beer to suit
every dining occasion and palate".
ED HUGHES

BEER STYLES
THERE IS A TYPE OF BEER TO SUIT EVERY PALATE AND EVERY OCCASION.

Essentially, there are only three types of beer in the world:

1. ALE
   Traditionally made using top-fermenting ale yeast.

2. LAGER
   Historically made using bottom-fermenting lager yeast and extended conditioning (lagering).

3. LAMBIC AND SOUR ALE
   Made by a method of spontaneous fermentation (or inoculated with a culture), using yeast but in big, open fermentation vessels, where bacterium and wild yeasts are encouraged to affect the beer and alter its flavour.

However, within these beer types there are at least 65 basic styles of beer available, which means there's bound to be something to suit every palate and every dish. Here are some of the most fundamental beer families that every beer drinker should know about. Within each family we've suggested a readily available classic that you should be able to pick up from your local supermarket, as well as a more unusual one that you might find in a specialist beer shop.

WHEAT BEER
Top fermented and brewed with a significant amount of wheat compared to the amount of malted barley, Wheat Beers tend to have long, thick, lasting heads, are a little hazy in texture and deliver a silky mouthfeel. Highly effervescent and usually light in flavour, they make great summer beers.
Widely available: Hoegaarden
Specialist: La Trappe Witte

LAMBIC AND SOUR ALE
Lambic and Sour Ale is usually wild fermented (in an open-topped vat so it's exposed to wild yeasts in the air), or inoculated with a culture – deliberately giving it an acidic, tart or sour taste. It can be aged for up to three years, allowing the wild yeast and bacteria to create alcohol and sour the beer.
Widely available: Thornbridge Tart
Specialist: Boon Oude Geuze

TRAPPIST BEER

Look for the Trappist hexagon marked on beers brewed within the walls of an abbey and overseen by Trappist monks. Ranging from golden to deep amber in colour, most Trappist Beers are Belgian and they are usually stronger than average ales, at between 5-12% ABV. Regularly categorised into Blonde, Dubbel, Tripel and Quadrupel varieties, this refers to how much of each ingredient is used during the brewing process.

Widely available: Westmalle Dubbel
Specialist: Rochefort 10

NEW WORLD PALE ALE

The style that inspired American craft beers, this is a wide category in the beer family. Pale to copper coloured, they are hop forward in style with tropical and citrus flavours that shine through.

Widely available: Sierra Nevada Pale Ale
Specialist: Pliny The Elder

TRADITIONAL IPA

So much more than a single style of ale, IPA (Indian Pale Ale) encompasses all sorts of hop forward beers. While accounts of its exact origins vary, it's widely believed that it gets its name due to being the Pale Ale shipped to India in the late 1700s and early 1800s. When Burton breweries dominated the IPA market in the 1830s, its popularity peaked. Then it almost disappeared in the second half of the 20th century, until a resurgence of craft beer rediscovered the style in the 1980s. While the style has altered hugely throughout its long history, traditional English IPAs boast the earthy and spicy flavours of classic Old World hops. White Shield probably has the longest lineage, tracing back to the strong Burton IPAs brewed in 1829.

Widely available: Worthington White Shield
Specialist: Bass

ENGLISH BITTER

Originating from brewers who wanted to differentiate their beer from milder brews, English Bitters use pale malts and more hops. Traditionally served in casks, but now often available in bottles, these golden and amber coloured beers are light bodied and usually low in fizz.

Widely available: Sharp's Sea Fury
Specialist: Sentinel ESB (Extra Sheffield Bitter)

PILSNER & LAGER

The most popular beer category in the world, encompassing mass-produced, big brand brews to complex and unique beers. From the soft, round tones of a German Helles to dry, crisp Czech Pilsners and everything in between.

Widely available: Staropramen
Specialist: Augustiner Helles

PORTER & STOUT

Think dark brown to black beers, mostly bitter with the malts giving off notes of toast, dark chocolate, coffee and roasted nuts. Oatmeal and Milk Stouts are the creamier, smoother types that are usually fuller-bodied and smoother.

Widely available: Guinness
Specialist: Bristol Beer Factory Milk Stout

As well as the key beer styles we could all be more savvy about, there are also some weird, wonderful and rare beers that might also cross your radar. These include SMOKED BEER, pumped with the aromas of wood-fired barley – the classic German Rauchbier version is a bit like a liquid smoked sausage (try the Schlenkerla Rauchbier from Bamberg). Also, with its roots in British brewing is BARLEY WINE, brewed from speciality malt that can be aged like fine red wine (try Robinson's Old Tom).

THE STORY OF BEER

FROM ITS ORIGINS TO ITS FUTURE

Every type of beer style has a story; whether it's an old English Ale from Burton-on-Trent (the historical home of British brewing), or a Trappist Beer brewed by Belgian monks. Just like wine, you can trace the style and origins of every beer and find out how it has developed over the years.

THE HISTORY OF BEER

Beer is arguably the oldest alcoholic beverage. It goes back thousands of years to when land was first cultivated. In its crudest form, beer is anything fermentable from starch. In ancient Egypt, hieroglyphics denote over 100 beer recipes, which were used as medicines and fermented using whatever crops were available – such as cassava root and millet. In Europe they used grain to brew beer. Until about 500 years ago, we didn't really use hops in the UK, instead we used ingredients such as nettles, gorse and heather to infuse flavour and aroma into beer.

LAGER

Lager is originally a German word that means storeroom or warehouse. The Germans were warehousing beers for years using ale yeast, long before lager yeast was even discovered in Bohemia. Consequently, up until the mid 1800s, all beer was probably top fermented or wild fermented. The Germans travelled and took their brewing skills and knowledge around the globe with them, hence lager becoming the most popular beer style in the world.

THE FUTURE OF BEER

In the last twenty years we've experienced huge developments in the production of beer styles, predominantly under the banner of craft beers. Along with a proliferation in the number of breweries, there has been huge enthusiasm for innovation, resulting in the emergence of new beer styles. However, there has also been a definite nod towards the heritage of beer and a movement towards producing more of the classic, traditional styles of beer: for example Barley Wines and the archetypal Munich Helles-style lager.

SUSTAINABLE BREWING

Stepping into the future, the challenges of brewing beer sustainably are key. As well as using as little water as possible and finding more eco-friendly transport methods, breweries such as Sharp's recycle the tonnes of malt and hops used to create beer, by using it as cattle and pig feed.

BEER TRENDS

In response to consumer demand, the brewing industry is becoming much more diverse and more varied beers are readily available. We're no longer brewing only standard 3.5-5% beers; beer can be anything from 2-22%. Low alcohol beers are increasingly popular, and there is also wider production of vegan and gluten-free beers.

A PINT-SIZED HISTORY OF SHARP'S BREWERY AND THE SECRET BAR

RACHEL WILLIAMS - COMMUNICATIONS MANAGER, SHARP'S BREWERY

Sharp's Brewery is a place of constant energy, where some awesome people come together to do their best work.

It isn't always an easy place to work - we are on the pursuit for perfection and never settle - but we share an entrepreneurial spirit and an unmistakable Cornish energy that comes from our location (where the land meets the sea) at the periphery of the country, which makes our brewery less a place of work and more a way of life. But while our work is a big part of life, it isnt the whole of life and being based in North Cornwall, our stunning surroundings are what refreshes us after a long week at work (as well as a beer or two).

We have seen swift business growth from brewing our very first pint of beer just over 20 years ago to, today, producing the UK's no.1 cask beer (Doom Bar)*. We are exceedingly proud of our success and our beers, but most of all our people, who, whether from Cornwall or enticed to the coastal lifestyle from elsewhere, are drawn to the energy of our brewery. We've been riding a wave... and what a ride it's been!

In 1994, when Bill Sharp founded the brewery in Rock, there was only a handful of other breweries in Cornwall (now there are around 40). Bill was a beer enthusiast and a highly ambitious character who focused on providing great quality beer and customer service. In 1995 Bill made a breakthrough by blending two of his original Sharp's beers; the malty Sharp's Own and the lighter, hoppier Cornish Coaster. These two beers combined to make a beer with just the right balance of malt and hops, the right abv at 4% and then, crucially, the right name (one which could not easily be forgotten). Doom Bar took off almost instantly.

In 2007, after a period of solid growth and the introduction of a very talented Head Brewer (Stuart Howe), near neighbour Rick Stein approached Sharp's about creating a beer to match his dishes, and after some trial runs at the brewery (with Chalky, Rick's beloved Jack Russell, in tow) a recipe was developed. Chalky's Bite, which we still brew today, is a Belgian style beer brewed with fennel and is our most awarded beer to date. It is also the beer that really ignited the passion in the brewery for pairing beer with food.

After the success of Chalky's ('Bite' was followed by 'Bark', a beer with ginger to complement Rick's 'Asian Odyssey' dishes) came the 'Connoisseurs Choice' range. This range was designed to enrapture the most discerning palate and the beers were bold in flavour, strong in ABV and received much critical acclaim from beer writers. We created beautiful stemmed glassware to elevate the beer and appeal to drinkers on different occasions, which kick-started a dialogue with some incredible chefs such as Alyn Williams and Nathan Outlaw on the possibilities of beer and food in a fine dining setting.

Today, the range of beers we produce at Sharp's is broader than ever, we produce around 1.5 million pints a week in Rock and we also have a small pilot brewery for experimentation. Head Brewer Andrew Madden's team brews beers in our signature, balanced and highly-drinkable style with Bill Sharp's motto: "We are only as good as our last pint", still driving the focus on consistency, which is, arguably, the hardest thing to achieve in brewing.

I have had many proud moments during Sharp's journey in beer and food – but none more so than the creation of this book, which has been a dream of mine and Ed's for a long time. We are super excited to share the next stage of our journey in beer and food with the people who matter most – you the consumers. Without people that enjoy our beer, and indeed the food created by the chefs, we as a food and drink industry wouldn't exist. So here's to you. And to the future of beer with food!

*CGA volume and value sales MAT to 14 July 2018

NICK WHITE
Brand Activation Manager Sharp's Brewery

One of the best things about my job is that rather than just talking about how good Sharp's beer is, I get to start conversations by offering them a taster – a great way to make friends easily!

My own part to play in Sharp's beer and food journey came soon after joining the brewery. Ed gave me an introductory beer tasting, and some kind of beer-soaked penny dropped. Ideas started to build in my head about how we needed to take him on tour to get people thinking about beer differently, and after a few 'beers and ideas' conversations with Rachel, the kernel of an idea for our 'Secret Bar' began to form.

By virtue of my theatre background, and love of creating surprises, the idea developed for the Secret Bar, which would be a wooden shipping crate that had been 'washed up on the Doom Bar sandbank' with no discernible way in. The intrepid few who did find a way in would be greeted with their own personal bar person, tasty morsels of stowed-away food and a new way to look at this wonderful pairing of beer and food.

The Secret Bar has now washed up at numerous events and gained us some incredible chef friends along the way, all of them as excited as we are about the possibilities of 'when beer meets food'.

SHARP'S TIMELINE

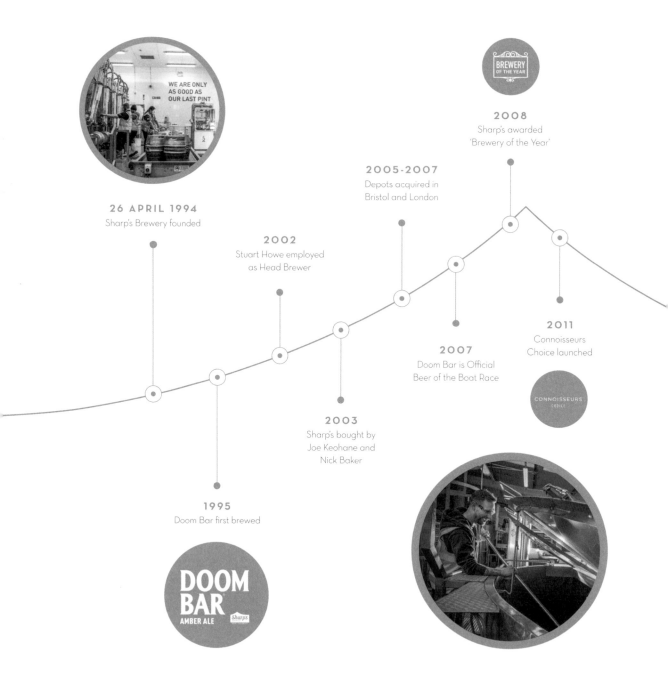

26 APRIL 1994
Sharp's Brewery founded

2002
Stuart Howe employed
as Head Brewer

2005-2007
Depots acquired in
Bristol and London

2008
Sharp's awarded
'Brewery of the Year'

2007
Doom Bar is Official
Beer of the Boat Race

2011
Connoisseurs
Choice launched

2003
Sharp's bought by
Joe Keohane and
Nick Baker

1995
Doom Bar first brewed

2013
Cornish Pilsner (now renamed 'Offshore') voted 'World's Best Lager' at the World Beer Awards

2015
Head Brewer Andrew Madden appointed after a worldwide search

2014
Sharp's and Nathan Outlaw join forces to open The Mariners pub

2017
Doom Bar becomes official beer of the British and Irish Lions

2011
Molson Coors acquires Sharp's and brings new distribution opportunities and investment to increase capacity and employee numbers

2013
Doom Bar becomes the UK's no 1 cask ale

2015
Sharp's takes on sponsorship of all the Blue Flag award applications in Cornwall

2016
Doom Bar becomes the UK's no 1 bottled ale

2018
Launch of Sharp's very first Cookbook!

THE BREWING PROCESS

MALT + HOPS + YEAST + WATER = BEER

BREW [broo]: To make (ale or beer) from malt and hops by infusion, boiling and fermentation.

MALT

Malted barley provides the sugars for fermentation, the nourishment for the yeast and infuses flavours such as biscuit and caramel. Sharp's Brewery uses only British malted barley, which is possibly the finest in the world.

HOPS

Hops are measured by percentage of alpha acid content. The higher the alpha acid content, the more bitterness they can impart into the beer. Most of the

bitterness in beer comes from hops, and how long they are steeped for. Like a tea bag, the longer you steep the hops for, the more bitter the beer becomes.

Germany's Hallertau region is the largest hop-growing region in the world. Just like with wines, there are Old World hop varieties and New World hop varieties. German, Czech, Slovenian and English hops are Old World. The US hops that are high in alpha acids, with tropical fruit aromas and high in bitterness, are New World types.

YEAST

| **Ale** | Traditionally made with top-fermenting ale yeast. |
| **Lager** | Traditionally made with bottom-fermenting yeast. |

WATER

Soft water is great for making lagers. The high quantities of gypsum in the water in Burton made the region famous for its IPAs. With brewing technology today, it is possible to recreate the flavour and content of water from a certain area, and therefore mirror the beer style from that region. For example, Pilsner was originally brewed only in the famous town of Pilsen in the Czech Republic, because its distinct flavour came from the clean, crisp water there. However, now Pilsners are brewed all over the world by recreating the water content of this famous beer-making region.

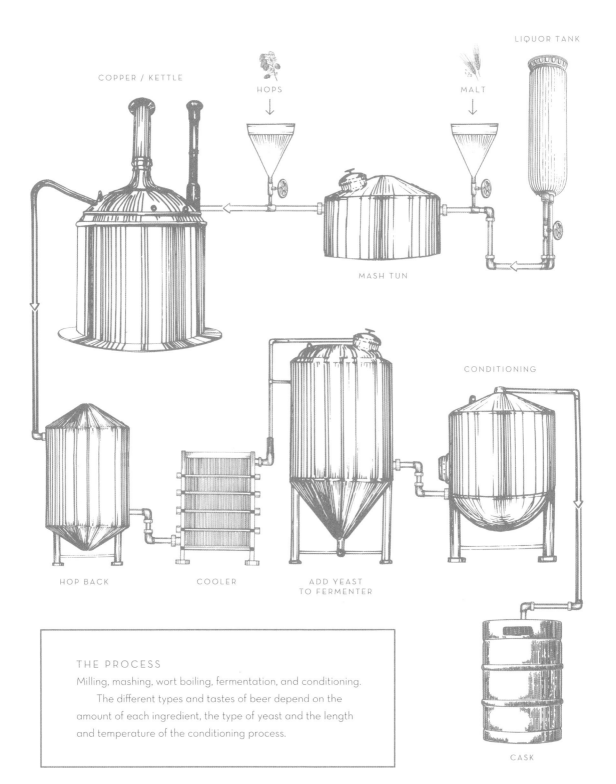

COPPER / KETTLE

HOPS

MALT

LIQUOR TANK

MASH TUN

CONDITIONING

HOP BACK

COOLER

ADD YEAST
TO FERMENTER

CASK

THE PROCESS
Milling, mashing, wort boiling, fermentation, and conditioning.
    The different types and tastes of beer depend on the
amount of each ingredient, the type of yeast and the length
and temperature of the conditioning process.

GLASSWARE

TRUST US, IT'S A GAME CHANGER

Using the right glassware makes a huge difference to the aroma, taste and presentation of beer, and how it's perceived. The pint glasses and straight-edged glasses that we're so used to don't deliver the optimum taste of the beer that the brewers have worked so hard on.

So we suggest serving beer in a wine glass or brandy balloon, half filled. This not only looks more attractive and commands more respect from the drinker, but the chalice shape of the vessel also accentuates the aromas and makes the beer taste better. Why? Because when the aromas are released, it triggers the olfactory nerve – which transmits your sense of smell to your brain. The majority of your sense of taste is controlled by this olfactory nerve, so the aroma hugely emphasises the taste of the beer.

When you're pairing beer and food, it's vital to understand and experience the full depth and flavour of the beer, so it needs to be served in the right glassware.

The Belgians are probably the most precise about their glassware, and have a huge variety of vessels unique to each brewery: for example, there's the beautiful Kwak hourglass and the Duvel chalice. At Sharp's we've also created beautiful stemmed glassware to go with our beers.

However, we don't want to confuse you with a daunting range of glasses to choose from – just make the simple change of serving beer in a red wine glass or brandy balloon. You'll taste the difference immediately.

These are some of the iconic glasses created for beers around the world:

NONIC   GOBLET

TANKARD   TULIP

PILSNER   WEIZEN

AL FRESCO

Easy to transport and wonderfully refreshing, beer is the natural addition to al fresco dining. So grab your favourite people, a few beers and some fresh, seasonal ingredients, and get outside.

WARM SALAD OF CORNISH GURNARD WITH TIGER PRAWNS

This is a great spring or summer dish. It's easy to do on a BBQ and goes very well with a beer. The flavours of the fish and the zing of the beer are a good marriage.

BY STEPHANE DELOURME

SERVES 4 AS A STARTER

2 thin gurnard fillets (approx. 100g each)

Olive oil

1 tbsp lemon juice

½ tsp peppercorns, crushed

½ tsp fennel seeds, crushed

½ tsp dried chilli flakes

12 raw tiger prawns, peeled

3 tbsp sherry vinegar

100g clarified butter

1 tbsp tomato concasse (peeled, deseeded and chopped tomatoes)

2 tbsp fennel herb, chopped

150g mixed salad leaves

Salt and pepper to season

PAIR WITH

Sharp's Chalky's Bite
Or a strong Belgian Pale Ale
or Belgian Abbey Beer

Mix the olive oil, salt, lemon juice, crushed peppercorns, fennel seeds and chilli together.

Add the gurnard and prawns to the dressing to marinate.

Sear the gurnard on a high heat for a few minutes on either side until lightly browned (either in a pan or on the BBQ).

Add the prawns and cook for 2 more minutes.

Remove the prawns and gurnard from the heat.

Add the sherry vinegar and the rest of the marinade to a little pan and heat through to warm up the dressing.

Remove the pan from the heat, then add the clarified butter, concasse, fennel herb and seasoning.

Cut the gurnard diagonally into slices and serve with the prawns and the salad, dressed with the sauce.

PORK RILLETTE WITH CIDER

Although I use Sharp's Orchard Cider when I make this in the pub, when Ed Hughes tried this dish he immediately saw its potential as a match for Sharp's Wolf Rock, and it soon became a feature in the Sharp's Secret Bar.

SERVES 10

1kg belly pork

2 tbsp wholegrain mustard

4 shallots, finely chopped

1 bunch parsley, chopped

2 tbsp duck fat

2 cloves garlic, finely chopped

Salt and pepper

2 tbsp lemon juice

For the poaching liquor

1 litre cider

2 bay leaves

3 sprig thyme

3 sprig rosemary

1 tbsp fennel seeds

1 tbsp star anise

1 whole garlic bulb, cut in half

1 tbsp whole peppercorns

2 carrots, chopped

2 onions, chopped

2 sticks celery, chopped

PAIR WITH

Sharp's Wolf Rock
Or an IPA or Amber Ale

BY HENK DE VILLIERS FERREIRA

Place the pork in an ovenproof dish, cover with the poaching liquor and cover the dish.

Cook at 140C for 3 hours, until soft and tender.

Allow to cool, before removing any bones and skin.

Meanwhile, reduce the cooking liquor to intensify the flavour. Then strain.

Sauté the shallots and garlic until translucent.

Chop the pork finely and add the shallots, garlic, chopped parsley, wholegrain mustard, lemon juice and duck fat.

Add some of the reduced liquor and mix well.

Place in a glass jar and set in a refrigerator.

This delicious rillette will last for at least a week, and will be at its tastiest after being refrigerated for a few days.

It's perfect served with our Doom Bar, Garlic and Rosemary Bread (p54) and Plum Chutney (p176).

HAM HOCK TERRINE WITH SALT-BAKED PINEAPPLE AND SPICED BREAD

This is the dish that keeps giving. It's perfect on its own, in a sandwich or crumbled in a soup.

SERVES 12

BY BEN PRIOR

For the ham hock terrine

2 pig's trotters

2 ham hocks, on the bone

2 shallots, peeled and chopped

2 tbsp baby capers, finely chopped

2 tbsp gherkins, finely chopped

2 bay leaves

1 tsp black peppercorns

1 tsp coriander seeds

750ml white wine

4 tbsp white wine vinegar

2⅔ handfuls of parsley and tarragon, finely chopped, reserve the stalks

3 sprigs of thyme

Sea salt and black pepper (freshly ground)

For the salt-baked pineapple

1 baby pineapple

10 cloves (approx.)

2kg coarse sea salt

1-2 tbsp Chinese five-spice powder

1-2 egg whites, lightly beaten

10g xanthan gum

For the spiced bread

100g milk

200g honey

For the ham hock terrine

Place the ham hocks and trotters into a large saucepan, cover with cold water, bring to the boil and boil steadily for 10 minutes, skimming off any scum, which floats to the surface.

Remove the hocks and trotters and discard the water. Return the hocks and trotters to the cleaned out pan.

Make a bouquet garni (bundle) with the bay leaves, thyme, parsley and tarragon stalks, add to the saucepan with the coriander seeds, peppercorns and shallots.

Pour in the white wine and 4 tbsp of white wine vinegar, adding enough cold water to cover and bring to a simmer.

Simmer very gently for approximately 2 hours, or until the hocks are tender and the flesh flakes easily.

Leave the hocks to cool in the liquid, then remove and cover with cling film (the trotters can be discarded). Strain the liquor through a piece of muslin into a clean pan.

Taste the liquor: if the flavour is not as strong as you like, bring to the boil and reduce. This will intensify the flavour but also increase its saltiness, so be careful and keep tasting. If you do reduce, pass it once again through a clean piece of muslin and into a jug.

Pick and shred the ham into nuggets. Place into a large bowl with the capers, gherkins and parsley. Mix well, taste and season with pepper.

Line a 1.5 litre terrine with a double layer of cling film,

RECIPE CONTINUED OVERLEAF...

HAM HOCK TERRINE WITH SALT-BAKED PINEAPPLE AND SPICED BREAD

150g rye flour

150g plain flour

75g brown sugar

25g baking powder

75g butter

2 eggs

1 lemon, zest

1 orange, zest

10g Chinese five-spice

PAIR WITH

Sharp's Atlantic
Or a Pale Ale or IPA

leaving some excess draping over the sides. Pile the mixture in and press down firmly. Slowly pour in the liquor – enough to just cover the meat – tapping down well as you do so to ensure it is spread throughout the terrine.

Cover with cling film and leave to chill overnight.

For the salt-baked pineapple

Heat the oven to 190C. Stud the 'eyes' of the pineapple with cloves.

Season the salt with the five-spice powder, then mix with the egg whites.

Pack the salt mixture around the pineapple to cover the skin completely.

Put the remaining salt into a baking tin and sit the pineapple on top.

Bake in the oven for 1 hour.

Allow to cool, then remove the salt crust and peel the pineapple.

Place in a blender with a pinch of five-spice and sea salt, then blend till smooth. Pass through a sieve and thicken with the xanthan gum.

For the spiced bread

Warm milk and honey together to dissolve, then cool slightly.

Mix all dry ingredients and the butter in an electric mixer.

Once combined, add the eggs followed by the milk and honey.

Once dough has formed, stop the mixer, put the dough into a well-oiled loaf tin and bake at 160C for 45-50 minutes.

Check a skewer comes out dry when inserted.

To serve, place terrine on the bread, add shavings of Cornish Gouda and a dollop of the pineapple.

NEWLYN CRAB TACOS

This fresh, zingy treat is perfect for a light lunchtime snack or as a starter.

SERVES 6

200g maseca flour

400g white Newlyn crab meat

2 tbsp yoghurt

1 jalapeño chilli, finely chopped

1 lime, juice

Salt and pepper

2 ripe avocados

1 clove of garlic

Splash of extra virgin olive oil

For the salsa

1 punnet San Marzano tomatoes, finely chopped

Bunch of spring onions, finely chopped

50g lilliput (extra fine) capers

Bunch of coriander, finely chopped

10ml white wine vinegar

50ml of extra virgin olive oil

PAIR WITH

Cobra
Or a Light Lager or a Pilsner

BY BEN PRIOR

Mix the maseca flour with warm water to form pliable dough. Make tacos from the dough and fry each one until golden.

Combine the crab meat, yoghurt and jalapeño together, then add the juice of half a lime, plus salt and pepper to taste.

Blend together the avocados, garlic and the juice of half a lime until smooth.

Make the salsa by mixing together the tomatoes, spring onions, capers, coriander, white wine vinegar and the extra virgin olive oil.

Pile your fillings into your taco and enjoy.

HERITAGE TOMATO SALAD

My grandparents were keen gardeners, so the smell of tomato plants and greenhouses takes me back to my childhood. Heritage or Heirloom tomatoes are one of nature's wonderful fruits and should be enjoyed at the height of the tomato season. This simple salad captures their delicious flavours.

SERVES 4

400g mixed Heritage tomatoes of various colours, cut into wedges, quarters and halves

60g red onions, diced

60ml olive oil

70g basil leaves, picked

Cornish sea salt

Freshly ground black pepper

PAIR WITH

Rodenbach Flanders Red
Or a Sour Beer, Pilsner
or Wheat Beer

BY ALAN BIRD

Mix the tomatoes, diced onion and olive oil in a bowl with seasoning.

Place picked basil leaves on top to finish.

FOURTH OF JULY DOG

Representing the Independence Day celebrations we had growing up in the US, this hot dog has all the essentials of a Fourth of July party: BBQ sauce, crunchy coleslaw and hopefully a beer to wash it down. All to celebrate the independence of the United States - and also the day when Will Smith saved us all from aliens.

SERVES 6

6 frankfurters (or your favourite sausages)

6 hot dog buns

For the southern-style BBQ sauce

300g French's Yellow Mustard

50g caster sugar

15g brown sugar

25g cider vinegar

70g water

Pinch of chilli powder

Pinch of cayenne powder

3g soy sauce

5g butter, cubed and cold

For the coleslaw

1 small cabbage, coarsely grated

2 carrots, coarsely grated

100g mayonnaise

55g caster sugar

45g buttermilk

10g lemon juice

22g white wine vinegar

3g salt

2g cracked black pepper

PAIR WITH

Franciscan Well Chieftain IPA
Or a New World Pale Ale or IPA

BY SANDIA CHANG

For the southern-style BBQ sauce

Mix all the ingredients in a pan, except the soy sauce and butter.

Bring the mixture to a gentle simmer and cook for 1 hour until the sauce is thick and is a dark golden brown colour. Whisk often during cooking to prevent the sauce from burning on the bottom.

When the sauce is thick and golden, add the soy sauce and the butter, mix well and take off the heat.

Let the sauce cool down. Once cool it can keep in the refrigerator for up to 5 days.

For the coleslaw

Make the coleslaw dressing by mixing the mayonnaise, caster sugar, buttermilk, lemon juice, white wine vinegar, salt and pepper.

Mix into the grated cabbage and carrot, then refrigerate. Best served fresh but can keep up to 2 days.

Assembling the hot dog

Squirt a good amount of BBQ sauce in the bun.

Place the hot dog in the bun and cover the top of the sausage with more BBQ sauce.

Top the hot dog with coleslaw.

KITCHEN GARDEN ASPARAGUS WITH BEURRE NOISETTE*

This recipe makes the most of fresh asparagus and new season herbs – I used everything I could find in my garden – mint, oyster leaf, basil, rosemary, thyme, oregano, sorrel and baby chard. I like to use a Big Green Egg BBQ for this recipe, but I've written it using a pan so it can be easily enjoyed anytime.

SERVES 2, AS A STARTER

12 freshly cut asparagus spears
80g unsalted butter
1 tbsp fresh garden herbs
Cornish sea salt
Splash of olive oil
½ lemon, juice only

PAIR WITH

Sharp's Atlantic
Or with a light Pale Ale
or Czech Lager.

BY ROSS GEACH

If you have cut your own asparagus they won't need prepping. However, if they are from a supermarket you may want to peel off the skin from the bottom inch to make sure they are not too fibrous.

Heat a non-stick pan with a splash of olive oil.

Add your asparagus, season with salt and sear until coloured but still al dente.

Remove the asparagus from the pan and put to one side.

Add the butter and keep moving the pan so the butter starts to froth.

Once you see the butter turning brown add the lemon juice and herbs.

Add the asparagus back into the pan and coat it in the delicious beurre noisette.

Pop the asparagus on the plate and give it a light sprinkle of sea salt flakes.

Decorate with more herbs and some edible flowers if you have them.

Make sure you have some nice bread such as sourdough to help mop up the nut-brown butter when you finish.

(*Beurre noisette translates as nut-brown butter)

ROSS GEACH

PADSTOW KITCHEN GARDEN
TRERETHERN FARM, PADSTOW

*Ross Geach supplies some of the best chefs
in Padstow with his delicious veg grown
overlooking the Camel Estuary.*

Ross Geach's family have worked the land on the stunning
Trerethern Farm for over 150 years. This sixth generation
farmer and former Stein's chef learnt his growing skills from
his grandfather and spent a decade in Stein's kitchens.

Renowned for his diverse and plentiful supply of
vegetables, Ross knows how to cheat the seasons and
offer chefs consistent produce from spring through to early
winter. Seasonal salads, kale, baby leeks and courgette
flowers bloom from March to November, while other unusual
varieties in demand include dragon's egg cucumbers,
kohlrabi and padron peppers.

Starting as a pot washer for Rick Stein and working his
way up to Head Chef, by the time Ross stepped out of the
kitchen and back into the garden in 2007, he knew exactly
what top chefs expected. "We can't grow beans as straight
as the Kenyans, but we package all of our produce so it's
ready to use and we ask the chefs exactly which parts of the
vegetables they want for their recipes." Ross explains.

Much of his garden produce is served in Stein's
restaurants from Padstow to Poole, and when Stein produced
an exclusive fennel beer, Chalky's Bite, with Sharp's, it was
fennel tops from Padstow Kitchen Garden that were used. A
huge foodie with a penchant for travel, Ross loves exploring
the cuisine in other countries, which influences what he grows.
Always experimenting with new varieties, he is currently
nurturing a crop of kale crossed with seaweed.

Now an authoritative nationwide figure on the topic
of gardening, Ross has supplied monthly columns to The
Telegraph, been featured in the Kitchen Garden Experts
book and appeared on Radio Cornwall's Gardenline,
Countryfile and The Hungry Sailors.

DOOM BAR, ROSEMARY AND GARLIC BREAD

We serve our Doom Bar bread at the beginning of a meal at Treviskers.

MAKES 1 LOAF

1kg bread flour

50ml olive oil

2 tbsp rosemary, roughly chopped

4 cloves of garlic, roughly chopped

50g fresh yeast

568ml Sharp's Doom Bar

250ml warm water

Salt

Olive oil and flaked sea salt

PAIR WITH

Sharp's Doom Bar on it's own, or ideally serve with the Pork Rillette on page 38 and Sharp's Wolf Rock IPA

BY HENK DE VILLIERS FERREIRA

Mix all the ingredients in a mixer with a dough hook for 9 minutes.

Let the dough prove until it's doubled in size.

Knock it back and roll flat into a baking tray.

Brush with olive oil and sprinkle with sea salt.

Allow to prove until doubled in size again.

Bake at 180C for 35 minutes, until golden.

Allow to cool.

WATERMELON, FETA AND MINT SALAD

The natural sweetness of watermelon makes it a treat to eat in the height of summer. The mint adds to the freshness and the feta with the lemon gives it a welcome zing of flavour.

SERVES 4

Taste the melon first and if it tastes as sweet as it should, simply discard the sugar from the recipe.

500g watermelon, skin removed

250g barrel-aged feta cheese, diced into even-sized cubes

100g mint leaves

50ml olive oil

40g caster sugar

Cornish sea salt

Fresh ground black pepper

1 lemon, juice and zest

PAIR WITH

Yeastie Boys Gunnamatta
Or a Wheat Beer

BY ALAN BIRD

Dice the watermelon into 1.5cm cubes and spread over a tray.

Sprinkle over the sugar and salt and leave for 10 minutes. Drain off the excess juices and place the melon into a suitable size bowl.

Add the diced feta and mint leaves.

Just before you serve the salad, drizzle over the olive oil and lemon juice and a couple of grinds of freshly ground pepper to taste.

You can add tomatoes and olives to this mix to enhance the flavours even more if you wish.

EVERYDAY MEALS

Whether you're short on time on a week night or preparing something to share on the weekend, everyday dishes can be savoured and enjoyed with a refreshing beer on the side.

FISH FINGER SANDWICH

Everyone has had a fish finger sandwich as a youngster. When I was at The Goring Hotel we used to make them every Friday for the staff. When I adapted the idea and put a posh fish finger sandwich on the bar menu when I opened Bird of Smithfield, it proved an instant hit.

SERVES 4

400g cod fillet, skinned and
cut into thin strips (or pollock,
hake, plaice, lemon sole)

2 eggs

100ml milk

100g flour

100g breadcrumbs

500g vegetable oil

200g frozen peas

15g mint leaves

50g butter

50ml vegetable stock

8 slices of sourdough bread

30ml mayonnaise
(homemade or shop bought)

40g gherkins, drained & finely diced

40g capers,
drained & finely chopped

1 small shallot, peeled, finely diced

3g flat leaf parsley, chopped

Seasoning

PAIR WITH

Pravha
Or a Pilsner, a Helles-style
Lager or a Dry Hopped Lager

BY ALAN BIRD

Break the eggs into a shallow tray and whisk in the milk.

Place the flour in a separate tray and season. Then place the breadcrumbs in another tray.

Dip the strips of fish into the flour, dust off the excess, then dip into the egg mix.

Shake off the excess and place into the breadcrumbs, coating the fish completely. Place these into the fridge to firm up.

Make the tartare sauce by mixing the mayonnaise, chopped shallot, gherkins, capers and parsley. Taste, season and put to one side.

Put a small pan of boiling water on the stove, adding any trimmings from the chopped shallot. Once boiling add the peas, boil for 2 minutes then remove from the heat and add the mint leaves.

Allow to cool slightly before draining off any excess water, keeping this to one side to add back if needed.

Blitz half of the peas and mint in a food processor or with a stick blender until smooth. Then add the other half of the peas and pulse to give them a rough chop. Add 10g of soft butter and test for seasoning.

Heat the vegetable oil in a fryer (or in a pan that holds twice the volume of the oil) to 190C. Test with a temperature probe, then carefully lower the cod strips into the oil and cook until golden brown. Remove from the oil and drain on some kitchen roll.

Butter the slices of sourdough bread and spread the pea purée onto four of them.

Place the fish strips on top of the pea purée. Spread the tartare sauce on the other four slices and place on top to make the sandwich.

Carefully cut these into halves and serve immediately.

VITELLO TONNATO PIZZA

I absolutely love pizza and this recipe is an all-round crowd pleaser – not too heavy and very fresh to eat.

MAKES 4 PIZZAS

For the dough

400g Shipton Mill OO flour

250g warm/tepid water

7.5g salt

12.5g dried live yeast

10g olive oil

For the bianca base

375g crème fraîche

125g garlic purée

½ lemon, zest – plus lemon juice to taste

20g chopped parsley

Salt to taste

For each pizza

1 dough ball

100g bianca base

150g buffalo mozzarella

20g red onions, sliced

5 cherry tomatoes, on the vine, sliced in half

2g dried oregano

5 slices of bresaola (air-dried, salted beef)

50g rocket leaves

1 fillet smoked mackerel

5 brined anchovies

Lemon zest and juice, to taste

PAIR WITH

Krombacher Pils
Or an Amber Ale or Pale Ale

BY JOHN WALTON

For the dough

Add the flour and salt into a mixing bowl, then add the olive oil.

Dissolve the yeast into the tepid water.

Slowly mix the flour, gradually adding the water and yeast mixture. Mix well for 10 minutes, until the dough is coming away from the bowl and is slightly firm.

Place a damp cloth on top of the bowl and leave to prove for 1 hour.

After an hour, knock the dough back and portion in to 4 balls. These are now ready for rolling out to make your pizza bases.

For the bianca base

Add the crème fraîche and garlic purée into a mixing bowl and whisk together.

Add the lemon zest and then juice to taste.

Finish with the chopped parsley.

Taste and season with salt if needed.

For the pizza

Using flour or semolina, shape your dough ball into a pizza.

Ladle the bianca base onto the centre of the rolled-out pizza dough and spread evenly to the edges, leaving 1-2cm around the edge for the crust.

Evenly top with the buffalo mozzarella, red onions, cherry tomatoes and oregano.

Using a pizza paddle, cook in a hot pizza oven at 250C (or slide onto a hot ceramic plate in a very hot oven) until the dough starts to blister. When you lift the base it should be golden and cooked on the under side.

Remove the pizza from the oven, top with sliced bresaola, pieces of smoked mackerel and anchovies.

Finish with fresh rocket, lemon zest and juice.

PADSTOW CRAB AND ST ENODOC ASPARAGUS TAGLIATELLE

This fresh summer pasta dish uses the best ingredients on my doorstep. It's best to make your own pasta, but if you're short on time just grab a bag of fresh tagliatelle from the shop.

SERVES 4

BY CHRIS MCCLURG

To make your own pasta

550g pasta flour

4 whole eggs with rich yolk (we like St Ewe)

6 egg yolks (rich yolk)

1 tsp salt

10ml extra virgin olive oil

For the rest of the dish

1 bunch green asparagus, peeled and sliced

½ red chilli, sliced thinly

½ green chilli, sliced thinly

4 spring onions, sliced thinly

200g fresh white crab meat

10ml olive oil

10 large basil leaves

20g pine nuts roasted

1 lemon, juice and zest

1 clove garlic, micro-planed finely

100ml fish stock

50g unsalted butter

To make your own pasta

Mix the eggs and oil together well.

Put the flour into a food processor with the salt, then gradually add your egg mixture until you've got a moist crumb texture (you shouldn't use all of the egg mixture, if you do the dough will be too wet).

Bring the dough together with your hands to form a ball.

Work the dough in your hands for a good 5 minutes, to give you stronger pasta dough, then wrap it in cling film and leave to rest in the fridge for at least 2 hours.

After a couple of hours, roll the dough through a pasta machine to about 3-4mm thick and cut into tagliatelle – or whatever shape you prefer.

Leave to dry slightly before adding boiling water to cook.

For the rest of the dish

Add the fish stock, butter and garlic to a pan and whisk to the boil.

Add the asparagus and cook lightly for 1 minute.

Meanwhile, put the fresh pasta in boiling water and cook for 2 minutes.

Add the chillies to the asparagus pan, then drain the pasta well and add that too.

Toss the pasta through the sauce and lightly fold through the fresh crab, leaving a little to dress the dish.

Finish the dish with fresh lemon juice and zest, and lightly fold through the chopped basil, pine nuts and spring onions.

Check the seasoning, top with the remaining crab and serve.

PAIR WITH

Brooklyn Lager
Or a Californian Common Lager
or a Dry Hopped Lager

BEEF STIR-FRY WITH UDON NOODLES

This delicious recipe is perfect for a quick lunch or supper to enjoy with your friends or family.

SERVES 4

4 rib-eye steaks, cut into ½ cm strips

2 packets udon noodles (fresh are best)

200g tenderstem broccoli, trimmed

200g cashew nuts, lightly toasted

50g sesame seeds, lightly toasted

20ml oyster sauce

20ml soy sauce

10ml sesame oil

1 bunch spring onions, washed, trimmed and sliced

PAIR WITH

Sharp's Sea Fury
Or a Red IPA or Best Bitter

BY STEVE MARSH

Seal the strips of beef in a nice hot wok, using the sesame oil to create a really nice flavour base to the beef, and adding a little pepper to season.

Blanch the udon noodles in hot water and add to the beef, cooking for around 4 minutes to get a nice even colouring.

Add the broccoli and sauces, continuously stirring, and add a little water at this point to help keep the noodles moist and give them a nice covering.

Evenly distribute the noodles, beef and tenderstem on four plates or bowls. Sprinkle over the sesame seeds, cashew nuts and – lastly – the spring onions as a garnish.

CRAB PASTILLES WITH FENNEL, APPLE AND CORNISH SEAWEED

Cornish crab and a fresh salad – the subtle, clear flavours of this dish make it perfect for a summer's evening.

SERVES 4 AS A STARTER

1 tsp vegetable oil

1 sheet spring roll pastry

100g fresh white crab meat, picked through and checked for shell fragments

1 tsp cornflour

2 tsp water

1 bulb fennel, with fronds – refrigerate until needed

Pinch of sea salt

Pinch of caster sugar

1 lime, zest and juice

200ml fresh, pressed apple juice

1 Granny Smith apple, cut into fine matchsticks

2 tbsp Cornish seaweed salad

PAIR WITH

Thornbridge Tart
Or a Light Lager or Munich Lager

BY KEN SYMONS

Make a paste with the cornflour and water, cut the spring roll pastry in half and brush with the paste.

Lightly season the fresh crab with a little salt and freshly ground pepper, divide into 2 and place on both pieces of pastry, to make 2 spring rolls.

Take the fennel from the fridge and remove the fine fronds (these will be used to decorate later). Using a Japanese mandolin, thinly slice the fennel bulb, add salt, sugar, seaweed salad, lime juice and zest, then mix together and place in the fridge.

Heat the oil in a non-stick frying pan, then fry the pastilles gently until golden all over. Cut in half so you have four small spring rolls.

Remove the fennel salad from the fridge and divide between 4 bowls, then add the remaining liquid to the apple juice and divide between the bowls. Place a spring roll on top, sprinkle with apple matchsticks and fennel fronds to serve.

WIENER SCHNITZEL

This favourite from my mother's Austrian heritage conjures up childhood memories of dining in the mountains with my family. Happy Days.

SERVES 4

For the schnitzel
4 veal escalopes (approx. 180g each)
2 eggs, beaten
100g plain flour
100g breadcrumbs
Salt and pepper
Clarified butter for frying

For the beef fat potatoes
2 large King Edward potatoes
200g beef dripping (or duck fat)
Thyme, garlic and caraway seeds

For the heritage tomato salad
360g heritage tomatoes
2 shallots
50ml white wine vinegar
50ml pumpkin oil
100ml rapeseed oil
50g toasted pumpkin seeds

For the hazelnut and caper butter
150g unsalted butter, chilled and diced
75g lilliput (extra fine) capers
50g roasted hazelnuts, roughly chopped
25g parsley, chopped
1 lemon, juiced

PAIR WITH
Duvel
Or a Lager or a Pilsner

BY DEZ TURLAND

For the schnitzel
Trim any sinew or fat from the escalopes, then pound until thin (5mm).

Dip in flour, egg, then breadcrumbs.

Pan fry in hot clarified butter for 2 minutes either side, then drain on kitchen paper and keep warm.

For the beef fat potatoes
Peel and dice potatoes into 1cm cubes.

Cook the potatoes until soft, on a very low heat in a saucepan with the beef fat, thyme, garlic and caraway seeds.

Turn up the heat and pan fry to colour.

For the heritage tomato salad
Cut the tomatoes and chill.

Finely chop shallots, mix with white wine vinegar and oils, and season.

When ready to serve, drizzle over tomatoes and finish with pumpkin seeds.

For the hazelnut and caper butter
Add the diced butter to a hot pan and cook until it starts to foam and you achieve a nutty brown colour.

Remove from the heat and squeeze in the lemon juice (which will stop the cooking process).

Add the rest of the ingredients and pour over your Wiener schnitzel.

PORTHILLY AND DOOM BAR MUSSELS

Mussels are one of my favourite shellfish, and paired with beer it takes them to a whole new level. This dish is a great centrepiece to any table.

SERVES 4

1kg Porthilly mussels, cleaned and de-bearded

1 red onion, sliced thinly

50g butter

200g smoked bacon

20g crème fraîche

1 bunch spring onions, sliced thinly

30g flat-leaf parsley, chopped

300ml Sharp's Doom Bar beer

PAIR WITH

Sharp's Doom Bar
Or a Wheat Beer or Czech Pilsner

BY JOHN WALTON

Slice the smoked bacon, add to a deep, hot pan and cook until golden.

Next add the butter, and once melted and nut brown in colour, add the sliced red onions and sweat lightly.

Now add the beer and crème fraîche and reduce slightly.

Add the mussels to the pan and stir well, then place a lid on top and steam until open.

Once the mussels are open, stir through the spring onions and chopped parsley, then serve straight away.

COCKTAILS
& CANAPÉS

Offer your guests something unique to get the party going. How about some moreish canapés matched with exceptional beers, or even some beer cocktails?

DBD (DOOM BAR DAIQUIRI)

BY ED HUGHES

A beery twist on a classic drink: the sweetness of the malt from the Doom Bar balances the acidity from the lime, and heightens the molasses and caramel in the rum.

MAKES ONE COCKTAIL

50ml golden rum
25ml lime juice
15ml sugar syrup
35ml Doom Bar
Slice of lime

Put all ingredients into a shaker with ice.
Shake hard for 10-12 seconds.
Strain, pour into goblet or Martini glass.
Garnish with a slice of lime.

LACTOM COLLINS

BY TRISTAN STEPHENSON

Beer is a massively unrecognised aperitif that can easily compete with the greats of the cocktail world – such as the Tom Collins. This recipe highlights the citrus, hoppy spices in the gin, fusing them with the acidity of a good sour beer. The trick here is to go sparingly with the beer, treating it like a fruit juice rather than a soda.

MAKES ONE COCKTAIL

30ml Tarquin's The Hopster gin

30ml fresh grapefruit juice

10ml sugar syrup

10ml egg white

Top up with a sour beer, such as Thornbridge Tart

Shake the first 4 ingredients with cubed ice.

Strain the liquid out of the shaker, discard the ice, then shake again to foam the drink up.

Pour the liquid into a chilled highball glass, top up with the beer and garnish with a strip of grapefruit zest.

THE
HOPSTER
COLLINS

BY ED HUGHES

One of my favourite drinks and perfect for a hot summer's day. The Hopster Gin (our collaboration with the Southwestern Distillery) uses specific hops that lift the citrus of both the lime and the beer. Make the individual drink or make a batch and serve in champagne flutes before a dinner party.

MAKES ONE COCKTAIL

35ml Tarquin's The Hopster gin
25ml lemon juice
15ml sugar syrup
200ml Offshore Pilsner
Twist of lemon

Add the gin, lemon juice and sugar syrup to a cocktail shaker, add ice and shake hard for six seconds.
Pour into a tall glass over ice.
Top up with Offshore Pilsner.
Garnish with a twist of lemon.

PEACH ALE SMASH

BY SANDIA CHANG

This cocktail is the perfect accompaniment for summer BBQs, picnics, or lounging in the garden. The colour and refreshing flavours remind me of iced tea - but this is definitely an iced tea just for adults.

MAKES ONE COCKTAIL

15ml Fino sherry

15ml RinQuinQuin peach liqueur

10ml lemon juice

Lemon slice to garnish

10ml sugar syrup

5 mint leaves

500ml Sharp's Doom Bar or Sea Fury

Add ice and all the ingredients - except the beer - to a cocktail shaker.
Shake well and strain into a Collins glass with ice.
Top up with Sharp's Doom Bar or Sea Fury.
Garnish with lemon slice and mint.

MEXICAN STREET CORN DIP WITH FLOUR TORTILLA CHIPS

Mexican street corn is served from tiny little steel carts all over Mexico. It is basically grilled corn covered with spices, cheese and mayonnaise. For the ease of serving at parties, I have converted the taste of the Mexican street food delicacy into a dip.

You can either serve this as a dip to share, or plated individually on chips for fancier parties.

MAKES 12 PORTIONS

340g fresh corn kernels cut off the cob, or drained canned corn

450g cheddar cheese, grated

160g pickled jalapeños, chopped

225g green onions, chopped

½ tsp ground cumin

½ tsp black pepper

177ml mayonnaise

227g sour cream

25g coriander, chopped

20g lime juice

Salt to taste

Flour tortillas, cut in to small triangles

PAIR WITH

Coors Light
Or a Pilsner or Pale Ale

BY SANDIA CHANG

In a skillet, heat the vegetable oil and sauté the corn kernels until slightly coloured. Put on a tray to cool completely.

In a large bowl, combine the sour cream, mayonnaise, cumin and black pepper.

Add the corn, cheese, jalapeños, lime juice, coriander and green onions to the sour cream mixture.

Season with salt to taste.

Stir until well combined and chill for at least 2 hours, or overnight for optimum flavour.

In a large pan, heat oil to 180C for deep frying. Drop in a few tortillas to fry, whilst stirring gently for even cooking.

Once the tortillas are golden, remove onto a paper towel to drain. Be aware that they cook very fast and they will crisp up when cooled.

Serve a dollop of the corn mixture on each chip to make canapés, or serve up alongside a bowl of dip for sharing.

PICKLED OYSTERS WITH CUCUMBER AND JALAPEÑO

This is one of Nathan Outlaw's classic oyster combinations that is a regular feature on our beer and food menu. If you don't like it spicy just leave out the jalapeños.

MAKES 3 PICKLED OYSTERS

3 Porthilly oysters

1 cucumber

1 large gherkin
(plus about 150ml juice
from the gherkin jar)

1 shallot

1 clove garlic

Dash olive oil

3 jalapeño chillis, sliced

PAIR WITH

Sharp's Camel Valley Pilsner
Or a Pilsner or Champagne Lager

BY ZACK HAWKE

Shuck the oysters and reserve the shells and juice.

Wash the shells out ready for later.

Place the oyster meat into the gherkin juice (so they are submerged) and leave for at least 2 hours.

Make your garnish by dicing the shallot and garlic very finely.

Dice the gherkin and cucumber into small cubes and mix with the shallots and garlic.

Add 1 tsp of the oyster juice and the olive oil.

When the oysters are ready, return them to the shells, dress with the garnish and place a jalapeño on top of each one.

LUKE MARSHALL

ROCK SHELLFISH
PORTHILLY FARM, ROCK

For shellfish farmer Luke Marshall, life and work revolves around the ebb and flow of the tides.

Bag a table at The Mariners in Rock and you can tuck into the finest local shellfish with a view to their source in the Camel Estuary. And it's not just raw oysters with Tabasco or lemon juice being served up these days. Luke's favourite is tempura with garlic mayo. "It converts people who wouldn't usually eat oysters as it changes the whole taste and texture of the product," he explains.

Porthilly Farm has been in the Marshall family since 1914. Luke's dad, Tim, started the oyster beds about 30 years ago, then selling most of his produce wholesale to France and Scotland. When Luke finished school he set up purification tanks to improve the quality of the oysters, enabling them to be sold to chefs. "When Nathan Outlaw got hold of the produce, demand went through the roof," said Luke. "We now supply Nathan Outlaw's, Paul Ainsworth's and Rick Stein's restaurants – some of the biggest names in Cornwall."

It's not only Outlaw's applaud that earned Porthilly oysters such a prestigious reputation. The Camel Estuary is rich in plankton and algae to feed the oysters, and the tides ensure the oysters are refreshed with clean Atlantic seawater each day. Baby oysters grow in floating cages, so the waves naturally chip the edges, promoting a deep-cut shape and meaty texture.

Some might say that the Porthilly mussels are also a cut above the rope-grown variety from other areas of Cornwall. Here they are grown in the riverbed, which makes them hardier and better fed as they soak up all the nutrients. "People love a bowl of moules marinière and a beer by the sea on a summer's day," says Luke.

SPICED CRAB ARRANCINI

My eldest son has a Sicilian godmother and I've been fortunate to work alongside some great Italian chefs over the years. They all love a great Arrancini. Apologies to all my Italian friends for the cardinal sin of adding parmesan to the breadcrumb mix, but it really does work.

MAKES 8-10 PORTIONS

100g carnaroli risotto rice

1 medium shallot, peeled and finely chopped

30g root ginger, scraped and crushed

1 clove garlic, peeled and crushed

1 red chilli, seeded and finely chopped

20g coriander leaves, chopped

50g olive oil

30g tomato puree

60ml white wine

200ml fish stock

200g brown crab meat

300g white crab meat

Salt and freshly ground black pepper

1 litre vegetable oil for frying

For the crumbing

100g panko breadcrumbs

100g plain flour

50g grated parmesan cheese

2 eggs

60ml milk

500ml vegetable oil

For the gremolata crème fraîche

1 lemon, zest

50g flat leaf parsley, picked and chopped

1 garlic clove, crushed into a paste

100g crème fraîche

Seasoning

BY ALAN BIRD

Gently cook the shallot, ginger, garlic and chilli in the olive oil until soft.

Add the rice and cook gently, then gradually add the tomato purée, sherry and fish stock and simmer until completely absorbed and the rice is just cooked. Add the crab meat and cook on a low heat for 3-4 minutes.

Season to taste and then leave to cool.

Refrigerate once cooled and leave to set.

Mould the chilled risotto into even bite - size balls, approx. 30g each in weight.

Meanwhile, set up 3 separate shallow trays for the crumbing: one for the flour, one for the crumbs and parmesan, and one for the egg and milk mix.

Add the balls to the flour, ensuring that they are fully coated. Shake off the excess flour, then place into the egg mix – again, ensuring that this coats the outside of the balls without any gaps. Then carefully place into the breadcrumbs and coat evenly.

Leave in the fridge to set.

To make the gremolata crème fraîche, mix all the ingredients together in a bowl and season.

Heat the vegetable oil to 190C in a deep fat fryer or a pan twice the size of the volume of oil. Check the temperature of the oil with a temperature probe.

Carefully place the crumbed balls into the hot oil and fry until crispy golden brown, then drain carefully on kitchen paper.

Serve with the crème fraîche. Take care as they will be hot inside.

 PAIR WITH

Sharp's Offshore Pilsner
Or a Lager or Golden Ale

SMOKED COD'S ROE DIP

From day one this has been one of the most popular dishes here at Outlaw's Fish Kitchen. So simple, but yet so tasty, it's great to have as a party treat or something to keep in the fridge for an afternoon snack.

SERVES 6 AS A STARTER, OR UP TO 10 AS A BITE

400g smoked cod's roe, rinsed and membrane removed

4 garlic gloves (unpeeled)

500ml olive oil

100g good quality crust-less white bread

100ml milk

40g Dijon mustard

2 lemons, juice

Sea salt and ground black pepper

Smoked paprika to sprinkle

Sourdough toast, to serve

PAIR WITH

Blue Moon
Or a Wheat Beer or Amber Ale

BY TIM BARNES

Heat the garlic and olive oil in a saucepan over a medium heat, until the oil starts to bubble around the garlic cloves. Turn the heat down slightly, so that the garlic doesn't fry, and cook gently for 20 minutes. When the garlic is soft, take the pan off the heat. Leave to infuse and cool completely.

Meanwhile, break the bread into chunks and place in a bowl. Pour on the milk and set aside to soak.

When the oil is cold, remove the garlic cloves with a slotted spoon and peel them, reserving the oil.

Put the cod's roe, mustard, lemon juice and garlic into a blender or food processor. Squeeze the bread to remove excess milk, then add to the blender and blitz for 1 minute. With the motor running, slowly add most of the garlic oil through the funnel until the mixture thickens and has the consistency of mayonnaise. Save some oil for serving.

Season with salt and pepper to taste and blend for another 20 seconds. Scrape into a bowl, cover and refrigerate until needed.

When ready to serve, sprinkle the dip generously with smoked paprika and drizzle with the reserved garlicky olive oil.

Accompany with plenty of warm sourdough.

CRISPY LING BITES WITH CHILLI JAM

Without a doubt, this dish is the all time Fish Kitchen favourite! It's perfect for any occasion, be it with a few beers or as part of a main meal.

SERVES 4 AS A STARTER, OR UP TO 8 AS A BITE

400g ling fillet, skinned and pin-boned

2 tbsp coriander, chopped

1 lime, zest, finely grated

½ tsp ground cumin

½ tsp cayenne pepper

100g gluten-free self-raising flour

120ml Cornish Pilsner (or similar beer)

1 litre sunflower oil for deep-frying

Sea salt and ground black pepper

For the chilli jam

1 red onion, peeled and finely diced

4 red peppers, cored, deseeded and finely sliced

6 red chillies, deseeded and finely sliced

3 garlic cloves, peeled and chopped

400g tinned plum tomatoes

300g soft brown sugar

150ml red wine vinegar

2 lemongrass stalks, tough outer layer removed, finely chopped

To serve

1 lime, cut into wedges

PAIR WITH

Sam Adams Boston Lager
Or a light Lager or Pilsner

BY TIM BARNES

To make the chilli jam, put all of the ingredients into a heavy-based pan and add a pinch of salt.

Bring to the boil, stirring to dissolve the sugar, then lower the heat and simmer gently, stirring occasionally, for about 45 minutes, until the jam is well reduced.

Once it starts to catch the bottom of the pan, stir constantly over the heat until it looks like bubbling lava. Transfer to a bowl and leave to cool. (Once cooled, the jam can be kept in the fridge for up to a week in a sealed container).

Cut the ling into rough 4cm chunks.

Mix the chopped coriander, lime zest, cumin, cayenne and a good pinch of salt together in a bowl. Add the ling pieces and toss to mix. Leave to marinate for 30 minutes.

To make the batter, mix the flour and beer together until smooth. Heat the oil to 180C in a deep-fat fryer or other suitable deep, heavy-based pan.

Season the fish with salt and pepper.

You will need to cook the fish in 2 or 3 batches: one at a time, dip each chunk into the batter to coat, then carefully lower into the hot oil. Deep fry for 3-4 minutes until cooked and crispy.

Gently lift the fish out and drain on kitchen paper. Keep warm while you cook the rest.

Sprinkle the fish chunks with a little salt and pepper and spear onto cocktail sticks.

Serve immediately, on a platter or individual plates, with a bowl of chilli jam and lime wedges on the side.

SMOKED HADDOCK RICE BALLS WITH CURRY MAYONNAISE

When I started working for Nathan Outlaw, my landlady, Annette (Ed Hughes' mum), first introduced me to kedgeree and it became one of my favourite things to eat. This recipe, inspired by that first kedgeree, is a great dish for any party.

SERVES 10

1 kg smoked haddock
600ml milk
30g curry powder
1 litre vegetable stock
250g carnaroli rice
100g parmesan cheese
30 coriander leaves, finely sliced
1 medium egg, beaten
150g plain flour
500g dried breadcrumbs
Salt and ground pepper to taste
Vegetable oil for deep frying

For the curry mayonnaise
500ml Rapeseed oil
50g curry powder
3 egg yolks
30g mustard
30g white wine vinegar

PAIR WITH

Little Creatures Pale Ale
Or a Smoked Beer or Dark Ale

BY TIM BARNES

For the smoked haddock balls

Bring the milk and curry powder to the boil. Adding the smoked haddock, bring to a simmer and cook for 2-3 minutes on a medium heat. Remove fish and set aside, discarding the milk.

Bring the stock to the boil. Add the rice with a pinch of salt and bring back to the boil. Lower the heat and simmer until the rice has absorbed all the stock.

Take off the heat and stir in the parmesan, coriander and smoked haddock, and leave to cool.

When cooled, roll the mixture into small balls, roughly the size of golf balls.

In a bowl, mix the beaten egg and flour together with salt and pepper until smoothly combined.

Place the breadcrumbs on a tray.

Heat the oil to 160C in a deep fat fryer or other suitable deep, heavy-based pan.

Pop the smoked haddock balls in the egg mix and then into the breadcrumbs, turning to coat all over. Deep fry in the hot oil, in batches if necessary, for about 2 minutes or until crisp and golden.

For the curry mayonnaise

Bring the rapeseed oil and curry powder to the boil, then set aside until cool.

When cool, strain the oil to separate the curry powder.

Whisk together the mustard, egg yolks and vinegar.

With a steady stream, pour in the strained curry oil, whilst constantly whisking until you reach mayonnaise consistency.

BEER SNACKS

Great snacks are a must when you're watching a match or catching up with your mates. Cook up a storm with these finger-licking snacks that are made to pair with beer.

CHILLI AND GARLIC NUTS

These nuts have a bit of a kick and make a great nibble at a party.

BY ZACK HAWKE

MAKES ONE SMALL BOWL FOR SHARING

200g peanuts

100g cashew nuts

1 large sprig of rosemary

1 tsp chilli flakes

4 cloves garlic, not peeled

1 tbsp cooking oil

2 pinches Cornish sea salt

PAIR WITH

Sharp's Doom Bar
Or a Czech Lager
or Pale Ale

Heat a heavy-based pan with the cooking oil on low heat, add the garlic cloves (whole) and rosemary sprig (also whole – so you can pick it out at the end) and cook for 8 minutes, stirring occasionally.

Add the peanuts and chilli and cook for 2 minutes, stirring pretty much constantly so the nuts don't burn.

Add the cashew nuts and salt, cook for a further 8 minutes, until the nuts are golden brown.

Pick out the rosemary and serve immediately, or let cool and keep in a jar for later – but they are best served warm.

SALMON SCOTCH EGGS

I chose this recipe for its wow factor. When you present these to your friends with perfectly cooked eggs, there isn't anything better!

MAKES 8

For the Scotch eggs

500g fresh salmon, skinned and bone-free

25g Cornish sea salt

25g caster sugar

30ml Cornish Orchards cider (or any other dry cider)

8 quail eggs

20g chopped coriander

20g sweet chilli sauce

1 dash Tabasco

10g lemon juice

½ lemon, juice and zest

50g fresh, dry mashed potato

4 egg whites

250g Japanese panko breadcrumbs

1 pinch ground white pepper

For the curried mayonnaise

100g mayonnaise

20g sweet chilli sauce

2 tsp korma curry powder

½ tsp turmeric

Lemon juice to taste

Salt to taste

PAIR WITH

Sharp's Atlantic
Or a Pale Ale or Wheat Beer

BY JOHN WALTON

Combine all of the mayonnaise ingredients into a bowl and whisk together, cover and leave to chill in the fridge until serving.

Mix the salt, sugar and cider together to form a paste, spread this all over the salmon and cover with cling film; leave to cure for 4 hours.

Once the salmon is cured, wash off the salt mix with cold running water, pat the salmon dry and place on a fresh cloth in the fridge until it is firm and chilled.

Dice the salmon into 1cm cubes.

Place in a bowl, add the coriander, sweet chilli, Tabasco, lemon juice, zest and pepper, and mix well.

Add the dry mash potato and mix together well, then cover with cling film and leave in the fridge to chill until needed.

Bring a pan of water to the boil, gently add the quail eggs, boil for 2 minutes and 15 seconds, then place straight into iced water to chill quickly.

After a few minutes carefully peel the eggs, then place them on kitchen tissue to dry.

Take your salmon mix from the fridge, place about 30g into the palm of your hand, pat it flat, place a quail egg into the middle and fold the mix around the egg to form a ball; add a little more mix if necessary.

Once you have made all your salmon egg balls, place them into the fridge to chill.

Once firm, dip the salmon balls into the egg white gently, one at a time. Keeping their shape, roll them in the crumbs to coat all over.

Now they are ready to deep fry at 180C for about a minute, or until they are golden and crispy.

Take out and cut in half straight away. Serve and enjoy with the curried korma mayonnaise.

GARLIC DOUGH BALLS

These are so moreish you won't be able to make enough of them for your friends.

SERVES 4-6

BY PAUL AINSWORTH

For the bread dough

450g strong plain flour

4g caster sugar

9g salt

255ml tepid water

12g fresh yeast

14g olive oil

For the garlic butter

2 bulbs of garlic

200ml olive oil

500g salted butter
(room temperature)

100g flat leaf parsley

Salt and pepper

PAIR WITH

King Cobra
Or a strong Lager
or Amber Ale

For the garlic butter

Peel the garlic cloves and place in a small pan with the olive oil, season lightly with salt and slowly cook the garlic until soft and tender.

Once cooled, strain off the oil and blitz the garlic in a food processor until smooth.

Add the soft butter to the garlic and mix really well.

Add the chopped parsley (retaining a little for garnish), mix well and season with salt and pepper.

Leave at room temperature.

For the dough

Add the yeast to the tepid water and olive oil, and mix to dissolve.

Put the flour, sugar and salt in a mixing bowl, then slowly add the water and yeast mixture, making sure the dough is always working – ideally with a dough hook on a food mixer.

Keep slowly working the dough until it is firm and not sticking to the outside of the bowl.

When the dough is ready, cover the bowl with a damp cloth and leave to prove until double its original size.

Now knock the dough back and roll into small balls (approx. 8-10g each). Pop these into an ovenproof dish and leave to prove once more until the dough has nearly doubled in size again.

Place into a preheated oven at 200C for 7-8 minutes until light and golden on top.

Remove from the oven and spread a good couple of tablespoons of garlic butter all over the baked dough, then return to the oven for a further 5 minutes.

Once the balls are coloured all over and have soaked up the butter, remove from the oven and finish by brushing over a little more butter, and sprinkling some chopped parsley and a good pinch of sea salt.

CHIPOTLE MAPLE CHICKEN WINGS

After spending many of my college years in California hanging out in sports bars, the memories of messy, spicy, sticky chicken wings and a pint of ice-cold beer are something I will never forget. My version of spicy chicken wings takes the smoky, spiciness of chipotle peppers and balances it with just a touch of sweetness from the maple syrup.

SERVES 6-8

1.5kg chicken wings
Cornflour for dusting
40g ketchup
100g golden syrup
30g maple syrup
110g cider vinegar
75g canned chipotle, finely chopped
30g Worcestershire sauce
1 tsp dry mustard
1 tsp onion powder
1 tsp garlic powder
Sour cream for drizzling

PAIR WITH

Franciscan Well Chieftain IPA
Or a New World IPA or Golden Ale

BY SANDIA CHANG

Mix all the ingredients together in a saucepan, except the sour cream and chicken.

Mix well, bring to a gentle simmer and cook on low heat for 30 minutes.

Take off the heat and allow it to cool.

Pat the chicken dry and toss lightly with cornflour.

Deep-fry the chicken until cooked through and crispy. If you don't have a deep fat fryer, half fill a deep saucepan with vegetable oil, heat to 190C and completely submerge the chicken wings, watching constantly. Remove carefully with metal tongs when cooked.

Whilst hot, toss the chicken in the chipotle maple sauce until evenly coated. Don't be shy with the amount of sauce.

Before serving, drizzle sour cream on top of the chicken.

Serve with lots of napkins and cold beer.

PORK CRACKLING WITH APPLE SAUCE

This classic bar snack is very popular at our pub, The Mariners in Rock. It's crispy, salty and great for pairing with traditional English ale. For this sauce, we use two different types of apples – the Bramleys fall apart to create a sauce and the Granny Smiths hold together for a bit of crunch!

MAKES A MEDIUM BOWL FOR SHARING

BY ZACK HAWKE

For the crackling

1 side of pork skin (you can get this from your local butcher)

3 tbsp table salt

For the apple sauce

500g Bramley apples

100g Granny Smith apples

25g caster sugar

4 tbsp water

½ lemon, juice

PAIR WITH

Sharp's Doom Bar
Or a traditional amber ale

For the crackling

Preheat the oven to 220C.

Lay the pork skin flat on a chopping board and use a good kitchen knife to score the fat at small intervals all the way across – horizontally, vertically and on both diagonals. Be careful not to go all the way through the skin. Flip the skin over and do the same again – this is a time consuming job but is very important.

Rub the salt all over the pork, making sure to get in every crack and crevice, then place in quite a deep, non-metallic container in the fridge for 30 minutes. You will be surprised how much moisture comes out of the pork skin.

Now wash the salt off the pork thoroughly and pat dry with kitchen roll. It must be absolutely dry.

Place the skin on an oven tray and put in the oven for 20 minutes – it will crackle and pop, so make sure you've got your extraction fan on before you take it out, and be very careful removing it from the oven as it will have leaked lots of oil.

Take out of the tray and pop on a resting rack so the excess fat can drip off.

For the apple sauce

Peel and dice the Bramley apples, pop in a saucepan and sweat with sugar, water and lemon juice.

When cooked out to a mush, blend them in a food processor (be careful blending warm foods as the purée may spit out).

Peel and dice the Granny Smith apples, return the purée to the stove and add Granny Smiths.

Cook on low until the Granny Smiths are just tender.

Pop into a sterilised Mason jar and the apple sauce will keep for 6 weeks. Alternatively, just keep refrigerated and use within a week.

HOMEMADE MUSTARD MAYONNAISE

BY ALAN BIRD

Making your own mayonnaise is one of life's simple pleasures and gives you a sense of great self-satisfaction. I serve this particular version with my Crispy Cornish Rarebit Bites.

150ml egg yolks

1 tsp water

25g English mustard

100g Dijon mustard

25ml white wine vinegar

1.125ml vegetable oil

375ml extra virgin olive oil

10ml lemon juice

Salt and pepper to taste

Place the egg yolks, water and mustards in a mixer or food processor and mix well on a low speed.

Add half the white wine vinegar, increasing the speed slowly and gradually adding the vegetable oil until it thickens. Add the rest of the vinegar towards the end and adjust with water if necessary.

Season to taste, add lemon juice to finish.

Keep in an airtight container in the refrigerator and use within two weeks.

CRISPY CORNISH RAREBIT BITES

I created this recipe when I was working with my friend Henk de Villiers Ferreira at Treviskers, where he serves delicious homemade snacks as an amuse bouche. I wanted to create a traditional English snack using Sharp's Seven Souls Dark Ale and it proved to be a huge hit – so have a go yourself and enjoy with a glass of the dark ale, too.

MAKES ABOUT 60 BITES

110g butter, unsalted

110g flour, plain

500ml Stout or Porter

400g Davidstow Cornish Extra Mature 18 month Cheddar

50ml Worcestershire sauce

60g English mustard

Seasoning

500ml vegetable oil

100g panko breadcrumbs

100g plain flour

2 eggs

60ml milk

BY ALAN BIRD

Melt the butter in a medium, thick-bottomed pan.

Add and stir in the flour, and cook gently over a low heat to form a roux. It should have a wet sand-like texture when ready.

Gradually add the dark ale until it becomes a thick sauce consistency, then add the grated cheese and allow to melt.

Add the Worcestershire sauce and, finally, the English mustard.

Taste and adjust seasoning to your taste.

Remove from the pan, spread onto a tray and allow to cool before refrigerating to allow to set.

Next make up your crumbing ingredients: mix the eggs and milk in one shallow tray. Put the flour in a separate tray, and the breadcrumbs in another.

Mould the rarebit mix into bite-size balls (approx. 20g) and place into the flour.

Shake off the excess flour before placing into the egg mix. Ensure they are well coated, and then place into the crumbs. Shake and move around in the tray to ensure they are all coated.

Heat the vegetable oil in a deep-fat fryer (or a pan twice the volume of the oil) to 190C.

Check the temperature with a temperature probe, before carefully lowering a few of the rarebit balls into the hot fat. Cook until golden brown and crispy, and carefully drain on kitchen paper.

Season lightly and serve with my Mustard Mayonnaise – see recipe opposite.

These can be frozen if not all needed at once.

PAIR WITH

Theakston's Old Peculier
Or a Stout or Porter

CRISPY PICKLES AND JALAPEÑO MAYONNAISE

An American inspired, simple beer snack and a bit of a guilty pleasure for the Sharp's team.

SERVES 2

8 gherkins
200g gluten-free self-raising flour
100ml Sharp's Offshore Pilsner
100ml carbonated water

For the mayonnaise

50g parsley
50g rocket
10 slices jalapeño chilli
30g grated parmesan
30ml white wine vinegar
10g Dijon mustard
Pinch salt
4 egg yolks
500ml vegetable oil

PAIR WITH

Sharp's Offshore Pilsner
Or any Pilsner or Lager

BY ZACK HAWKE

Mix the beer, water and flour into a thick batter.

Dip the gherkins into the batter and drop into a pre-heated fryer at 180C.

When they are puffed up and crispy, remove with a slotted spoon and place on kitchen paper to drain.

To make the mayonnaise, pop the rocket, parsley, jalapeño, parmesan, mustard and egg yolks into the blender.

Blend for 1 minute until smooth, then add the vinegar.

With the blender on low, slowly trickle in the oil until the mayonnaise becomes thick.

Add the salt and check the taste – it may need a little more.

Suggestion

You don't have to use gherkins here. Just replace with your vegetable of choice.

SAUSAGES IN CANDIED BACON WITH MULLED CRANBERRY KETCHUP

This sweet and succulent dish is always a winning snack or light lunch at our Christmas festivals and events – and also great served as a canapé.

SERVES 4 AS A SIDE OR CANAPÉ

8 large chipolata sausages

8 large slices smoked streaky bacon

170g light brown sugar

Black pepper, to taste

For the mulled ketchup

200g fresh cranberries

50ml port

1 tsp cinnamon

1 tsp nutmeg

1 orange zest and juice

2 star anise

1 tsp grated root ginger

30-50g light brown or caster sugar (add more or less according to your taste)

Knob of butter

PAIR WITH

Boon Oude Geuze Sour Ale
Or an IPA or Pale Ale

BY NICK ARCHER

Add the cranberries and butter to a crockpot or sturdy saucepan on a high heat. Stir well until the cranberries are popping and hissing. Add the grated ginger, sugar and port and stir well for about 5 minutes.

Reduce the heat to a simmer and add your mulled spices/ flavours. Use a wooden spoon to push down on the cranberries and break them up, adding a little water if needed to stop it sticking, then simmer for 10-15 minutes. Taste and add more sugar and seasoning if required.

Use either a hand blender or potato masher to break down the cranberries further and allow to cool. You can store this in the fridge, in an airtight container, for up to 14 days.

Pour the sugar and black pepper into a bowl and tip in the streaky bacon, then mix well until the bacon is covered. Wrap each slice of bacon around a sausage, completely covering up the sausage.

Place on a baking tray and cook at 150C for 20 minutes. It may take a bit longer for the bacon to crisp up, so bake for longer if necessary, but don't turn the temperature up.

Place the delicious pigs in candied blankets on a serving platter with a bowl of your mulled cranberry ketchup and get dipping!

ROASTS

Sundays are made for roasts – a meal that tastes especially good after an invigorating coastal walk. There's a beer to match every roast dinner, whether it's a delicate Pilsner with lighter dishes , or a darker malty beer with roast beef.

113

MICHELADA

Can't decide between a beer and a Bloody Mary? Then try a Michelada. This drink originates from Mexico and tastes something like spicy salsa mixed with beer. My recipe uses beef stock and sweet Madeira to bolster savoury, umami notes, transforming the drink into a lighter, brighter rendition of the Bloody Mary formula.

MAKES ONE COCKTAIL

15ml sweet Madeira
15ml beef stock
10ml lime juice
1g salt
Tabasco (according to taste)
Top up with Sharp's Wolf Rock

BY TRISTAN STEPHENSON

Wet the rim of a tall glass with lime juice, then carefully dip the outside into flaked Cornish sea salt.

Add the Madeira, stock, lime, salt and your preferred amount of Tabasco to the glass and give it a good stir.

Top up with the beer and serve immediately.

ROAST RIB OF DEXTER BEEF

This hearty roast served with seasonal veg is a fantastic feast to be enjoyed with family and friends.

SERVES 8

1 whole rib Dexter beef
(approx. 8kg), 28-day matured

2kg Jersey Royals, washed

2 bunches rainbow carrots, washed

1 medium celeriac, washed
and peeled

1 red onion

1 litre beef stock

500g tenderstem broccoli

2 bunches Cornish asparagus
(trim off the woody stalks)

2 bulbs garlic, broken into cloves

1 bunch rosemary

1 bunch thyme

PAIR WITH

Sharp's Sea Fury
Or a Best Bitter or ESB
(Extra Special Bitter)

BY STEVE MARSH

Seal the beef in a nice big frying pan with a little oil. Seal both ends, then the top (where most of the fat is), to release a little fat for it to cook in.

Place the beef on a roasting tray and put in the oven at 180C. Cooking time depends on how pink you want the meat to be – about 1½ hours cooking plus 20 minutes resting time will achieve a 'medium' cook.

Use a large roasting pan for the vegetables and potatoes. Cut the Jersey Royals and celeriac into mouth-sized pieces, mix together with the garlic and sliced red onion, drizzle with a little oil and season with salt and pepper.

Add some thyme and rosemary, then put the tray in the oven about 25 minutes before the beef is ready to come out. Every 10 minutes give the vegetables a stir so that they cook evenly.

Blanch the asparagus and broccoli in boiling (seasoned) water just before you serve the meal – if you add some butter to your blanching water before you cook the vegetables, it will give the veg a lovely sheen and improve the taste.

Every roast needs some lovely gravy, so make your own using a nice beef stock, or buy a decent supermarket gravy.

Serve up, sit down and enjoy with your friends and family, and a glass of beer.

BURRATA, ROASTED PUMPKIN AND ROMESCO SAUCE

This dish is a great winter warmer; the sweet earthy squash and creamy burrata work wonderfully together.

SERVES 4

1 pumpkin, peeled

4 balls of Italian burrata
(1 per person)

For the romesco sauce

20g toasted white bread

3 red peppers

200g ripe tomatoes

30g blanched almonds

30g blanched hazelnuts

2 cloves garlic

2 tbsp sherry vinegar

PAIR WITH

Sharp's Chalky's Bite
Or a Wheat Beer

BY ZACK HAWKE

Preheat oven to 180C.

Roast, then peel the red peppers and tomatoes and set aside.

Slice the pumpkin into finger-size pieces, place on a baking tray with a little oil and roast until tender.

Roast the nuts for about 5 minutes until brown.

Blitz the peppers, tomatoes, nuts and the rest of the romesco ingredients in the blender, adding a pinch of salt to taste.

Season the burrata with salt and black pepper.

Put a dollop of the sauce on the plate, arrange the squash on the sauce and top with the burrata.

ROAST SHOULDER OF PORK WITH CRISPY CRACKLING

Shoulder of pork is great for roasting, as you get nice delicate flesh, just the right amount of fat through the middle and the perfect, crispy crackling.

SERVES 6 HUNGRY PEOPLE

2kg boned and rolled shoulder of free-range pork (ask your butcher to score the skin)

2 large pinches Cornish sea salt

Splash of cooking oil

PAIR WITH

Leffe Blonde
Or an IPA or a Honey Beer

BY ZACK HAWKE

It's best to start the prep the night before: uncover the pork and rub with a little oil all over the skin. Sprinkle with the Cornish sea salt and leave unwrapped in the fridge overnight – this will help to draw out some moisture from the skin and give you good crackling.

Take the pork out of the fridge about 30 minutes before you want to cook it, place it on a wire rack on the tray that you want to cook it on and leave at room temperature.

Preheat the oven to 220C and cook the pork for 20 minutes, before turning the oven down to 180C and cooking for a further hour. This method gives you better crackling.

Let the pork rest for 20 minutes in a warm place before you start to carve it.

It's best to remove all of the crackling from the joint before carving, and share out the crispy crackling.

STEPHANE DELOURME

HEAD CHEF
THE SEAFOOD RESTAURANT, PADSTOW

Growing up in Quiberon, Brittany, Head Chef Stephane Delourme has a natural passion for seafood and the coast.

When Stephane Delourme decided it was time to swap city life for the coast, he followed his Celtic roots – and his wife – to Cornwall. He'd already worked his way around half a dozen Michelin-starred restaurants in Paris, London and Dublin, always trying to focus his cooking around his love of seafood. Once in Cornwall, he soon stepped into Paul Ripley's shoes as the Head Chef of Stein's flagship Seafood Restaurant, where he's been manning the kitchen for over 20 years.

"I've loved fish and shellfish ever since I was little," says Stephane. "At home in Brittany we'd always eat Fruits de Mer instead of a Sunday roast." Fortunate to combine the coastal lifestyle with a high profile cheffing career, he says: "The Seafood Restaurant is an amazing place to work, because it's got the buzz and reputation of a top London restaurant, yet it's in one of the most beautiful seaside resorts in the world."

Stephane's relationship with Sharp's was sparked in 2006, when Stein worked with the brewery to develop the unique fennel beer, Chalky's Bite, to go with seafood. Now beer and food matching has become part of the dining experience at The Seafood Restaurant. "Beer drinking is part of the British DNA, and there are all sorts of different beers that work wonderfully with our seafood dishes," says Stephane. "There's been a huge development in beer styles and flavours in recent years, and just as the foodie industry has mushroomed in the last decade, now the beer industry is evolving to catch up. People are becoming more adventurous, trying different flavours, and being more open-minded about beer."

Take a seat at The Seafood Restaurant for a platter of Porthilly Oysters and glass of a Camel Valley Pilsner, and it's plain to see that world-class seafood and beer go hand-in-hand – especially by the sea.

HAKE WITH PANCETTA, POINTED CABBAGE AND DOOM BAR

Cornish wild hake is plentiful and good value. The soft, sweet flesh of the fish is offset by the bitterness of the Doom Bar ale, and works well with the creamy sauce and earthiness of the pancetta. This dish has everything - fish, vegetables and beer.

SERVES 4

4 hake fillets (approx. 160g each)

50g salted butter

3 tsp salt

½ tsp sugar

5 grates of nutmeg (pass the nutmeg over the grater five times)

2 Hispi cabbages (sweet, pointed cabbages)

1 carrot, sliced into triangles

40g banana shallots, finely chopped

100g pancetta

10g flat leaf parsley, chopped

For the sauce

250ml Doom Bar ale

700ml chicken stock

100g salted butter

30g double cream

1 lemon, juiced

10g whipped cream

For the gremolata

100g flat leaf parsley

Salt

Black pepper

30g garlic, finely chopped

½ lemon juice

1 lemon zest

200g olive oil

20g pumpkin seeds

BY STEPHANE DELOURME

Remove the outer leaves of the cabbage. Cut in half, remove the solid stalk and thinly slice.

Melt 50g of butter in a saucepan over medium heat, then add the salt, sugar, nutmeg, cabbage, carrots and shallots. Put a lid on the pan and cook for 5-10 minutes, stirring frequently to prevent the cabbage from catching.

For the sauce, reduce half the Doom Bar until it almost catches on the bottom of the pan and deglaze with the remaining half. Then add chicken stock and reduce by two thirds. Add the butter, double cream and lemon juice.

Sear the hake fillets for 2 minutes on each side until golden.

Cook the pancetta in the oven at 100C, until crispy and golden.

Stir the chopped parsley into the warm cabbage.

Add the whipped cream to the warm sauce.

Mix together the gremolata ingredients, to be served at room temperature.

Place the cabbage on the plate, the hake on top, pour the sauce around it and garnish with the crispy pancetta and gremolata.

 PAIR WITH

Sharp's Doom Bar
Or an Amber Ale or Wheat Beer

BEER YORKSHIRE PUDDINGS

BY HENK DE VILLIERS FERREIRA

Sunday roast is a big deal for us. We've had a lot of practise making Yorkshire Puddings and this recipe will never fail you. I use Sharp's Coaster but any golden, light ale will do.

MAKES 24 YORKSHIRE PUDDINGS

8 medium eggs
500g plain flour
568ml golden, light ale
Salt and pepper
Beef dripping (just enough to line Yorkshire tray)

Mix the ingredients – except the beef dripping – with a whisk and allow to cool in a refrigerator.

Cover the base of each mould of a Yorkshire tray with the beef dripping and heat at 220C.

Once the tray is smoking hot, quarter-fill each pudding slot with batter mix.

Bake in the hot oven for 18 minutes.

CARROTS AND TARRAGON

BY ZACK HAWKE

Sweet, earthy carrots go really well with the anise flavour in the tarragon, making these the perfect accompaniment to the fabulous Sunday lunch at The Mariners.

SERVES 4-6

6 large British
carrots, peeled

Small bunch of tarragon

150g unsalted butter

150g brown sugar

Cornish sea salt

1 star anise

Slice the carrots in half, and then quarter them long ways to make 8 batons from each carrot.

Place the carrots in a pan and add the butter, sugar, tarragon (including the stalks), a good pinch of salt and star anise.

Add just enough cold water to cover the carrots.

Cook on low with a lid on, until the carrots are tender.

Remove the carrots with a slotted spoon and keep warm in a bowl.

Turn the heat up and reduce the cooking liquor until it is thick and syrupy, then pass through a sieve and toss the carrots through it.

CHEESY LEEKS

Cheesy leeks have been on the Sunday lunch menu at The Mariners for four years now and are a firm favourite with our diners.

SERVES 4-6

2 leeks, washed and
outer leaves removed

50g butter

50g plain flour

1 litre milk

150g Davidstow cheddar, grated

2 pinches Cornish sea salt

1 tsp Worcester sauce

1 tbsp English mustard

50g breadcrumbs

1 pinch chopped chives

BY ZACK HAWKE

Preheat oven to 180C.

Trim the tops and bottoms off the leeks and slice them into thin rounds.

Melt the butter in a saucepan, add the flour and stir on low for 1-2 minutes, then add one third of the milk and stir until it becomes thick and smooth.

Add the next third of milk and stir until thick; repeat with the final third of milk and let it cook on low for 5 minutes.

Add a pinch of salt, the Worcester sauce, the mustard and 100g of the cheese. Taste it – it may need more salt.

In a frying pan, sweat the leeks off on a low heat until fully cooked, place in a sieve and squeeze out any excess moisture.

Mix the leeks and sauce and pop in an oven dish, sprinkle with the breadcrumbs first (this stops them burning), then sprinkle with the rest of the grated cheese.

Bake for 30 minutes until golden brown on top and piping hot in the middle.

Sprinkle with the chives just before serving.

CHOCOLATE PECAN TART WITH HORLICKS ICE CREAM

This pecan tart recipe was given to me by a customer who was staying in a hotel where I once worked in London. I took out the blue cheese and added the chocolate – and I think it works a lot better now.

SERVES 4

BY STUART PATE

For the pecan tart

200g sweet pastry

120g golden syrup

20g butter

200g demerara sugar

⅛ tsp salt

¼ tsp vanilla extract

150g dark chocolate

200g eggs

200g pecan nuts, chopped

4 x 9cm round tart tins

For the Horlicks ice cream

500g milk

500g double cream

30g glucose

140g egg yolk

75g sugar

75g light brown sugar

60g Horlicks

For the garnish

15g gold chocolate dust

15g crushed biscuit crumbs

25g caramelised pecan nuts

PAIR WITH

Bristol Beer Factory Milk Stout
Or a Porter or Barley Wine

For the pecan tart

Heat the butter, sugar, golden syrup, salt and vanilla in saucepan.

Pour onto the chocolate and mix until melted.

Cool to blood temperature and add the egg, mix thoroughly.

Fold in the chopped pecans.

Chill.

Line your pastry tins with sweet pastry rolled out to 2mm thickness and prick each pastry case with a fork.

Fill with the chocolate pecan tart mix and bake at 185C for 20-25 minutes.

For the Horlicks ice cream

Bring the milk, cream and glucose to a simmer.

Whisk together the egg yolk, sugar and Horlicks.

Pour the milk mixture onto the eggs and whisk to mix. Then return to the heat.

Cook for 5 minutes on a low heat (83C), while whisking constantly.

Strain, cool over ice and freeze in an ice cream machine once completely chilled.

Serve the tart with ice cream and garnish.

SHARP'S BEERAMISU

The beeramisu came around a few years back when my sous chef was playing around with Sharp's Dubbel Coffee Stout. The beer works more like a fortified wine in certain recipes rather than a beer, and with the coffee element it was perfect. The dish became a best-selling dessert that still makes an appearance on special occasions.

SERVES 4

For the base

100g Savoiardi biscuits

100ml good Chocolate Stout or Porter with a fairly high ABV

For the cream

50ml Chocolate Stout or Porter (as above)

125g mascarpone

250ml double cream

1 orange, zest

2 tbsp demerara sugar

For the ganache

75g chocolate (70% dark chocolate)

15g butter

1 tbsp Chocolate Stout or Porter (as above)

100ml double cream

For the garnish

Orange zest

Cocoa powder

PAIR WITH

Guinness West Indies Porter
Or an Imperial Stout

BY ZACK HAWKE

This seems complicated, but all you're doing is making the layers for a tiramisu. Make each stage in a separate bowl, and then layer them in a glass dish.

Soak the finger biscuits in the Stout/Porter.

Whip up all the cream ingredients in a separate bowl.

Put all the ganache ingredients, except the cream, in a heatproof bowl.

Bring the cream to the boil in a separate pan and pour over the other ganache ingredients. Mix well into a thick chocolate sauce consistency.

Layer into a dish with sponge at the bottom, then cream, then ganache – do this as many times as you can. Then dust with a generous amount of cocoa and a pinch of orange zest.

CELEBRATIONS

Celebrate life's special events with these fabulous recipes. Whether it's a dinner party or a birthday, make these delicious food and beer pairings part of the occasion.

135

Choose from two fabulous, three-course dinner party menus by Jude Kereama and Alyn Williams. Plus a stunning showstopper by Stuart Pate.

DINNER PARTY ONE

BY JUDE KEREAMA

STARTER
SINGAPORE CRAB BAO BUN

SERVES 4

This dish is a take on Singapore crab, but served inside a bao bun. The citrusy notes of Sharp's Offshore Pilsner go perfectly with seafood and the grassy notes of the beer also match the Asian flavours of coriander and lime. Be sure to make plenty, as these are very moreish.

For the deep-fried soft shell crab

4 soft shell crabs

200ml buttermilk

1 tbsp Szechuan pepper

1 tbsp Cornish sea salt

250g plain flour

For the bao buns

(This makes 24 bao buns, which can be frozen for future use once cooked.)

3g dried yeast

170ml warm water

25g sugar

½ tsp vegetable oil

¼ tsp baking soda

¼ tsp baking powder

½ tsp salt

300g strong flour

Vegetable oil for brushing

For the Singapore chilli sauce

10 large dried red chillies, rehydrated, deseeded and diced (we like Szechuan long-dried chilli)

5 serrano chillies, diced

1 tbsp shrimp paste, roasted in the oven for 5 minutes

1 thumb of galangal, diced

1 stick lemongrass, diced

25ml vegetable oil

For the deep-fried soft shell crab

Soak the soft shell crabs in the buttermilk.

Toast off the Szechuan pepper in a frying pan for about a minute and then let cool down.

Grind the pepper with the salt and then season the flour.

When needed, take each crab and let the excess buttermilk drip off, then dredge in the flour to coat.

Deep-fry at 180C till crispy.

For the bao buns

Mix the water, sugar, vegetable oil and dried yeast in a mixing bowl and leave to react.

Mix all the other dry ingredients together.

When the yeast is activated, add everything together to make a dough.

Knead for a good 10 minutes and then cover with a damp cloth and leave in a warm place to prove for about 1½ hours.

Knock the dough back and divide into about 24 even balls.

Leave to prove for another 30 minutes.

In the meantime, cut out 24 greaseproof paper squares (approx. 10 x 10cm).

When the dough balls are ready, roll them out into ovals. Take an oiled chopstick and place in the middle of the ovals, fold over the ovals to make a bao shape and then withdraw the chopstick.

Place on the greaseproof paper and let rise for another 30 minutes. When ready, steam the buns in batches for 10 minutes.

RECIPE CONTINUED OVERLEAF...

STARTER
SINGAPORE
CRAB BAO
BUN

1 banana shallot, diced

3 cloves garlic, crushed

1 tbsp ginger, chopped

3 tbsp tomato ketchup

1 tbsp black bean sauce

1 tbsp sugar

¼ tsp salt

3 spring onions, chopped

2 tbsp coriander, chopped

For the Asian slaw

100g chopped Chinese cabbage

100g carrot, julienned
(grated into matchsticks)

3 spring onions, chopped

25g coriander, chopped

4 tbsp mirin

1 tbsp brown muscovado sugar

60ml rice wine vinegar

1 tsp golden sesame oil

1 tsp light soy sauce

1 lime, juice

For the seaweed mayo

2 nori sheets

200g mayonnaise

½ lemon, juice

To garnish

Coriander micro-cress (or the
picked leaves of bigger coriander)

1 lime, wedges

12 slices of cucumber

For the Singapore chilli sauce

Mix the chillies, shrimp paste, galangal and lemongrass together and blend to make a paste.

Sauté the banana shallot, garlic and ginger in the vegetable oil and cook until golden. Add in the chilli paste, tomato ketchup, black bean sauce, sugar and salt.

Take off the heat and add the spring onions and coriander.

For the Asian slaw

Pop the cabbage, carrots, spring onions and coriander in a bowl.

Combine the rest of the ingredients to make the dressing and toss through the chopped vegetables.

For the seaweed mayo

Dry the nori sheets in a cool oven until very crisp and then blitz into a powder.

Season the mayonnaise with the lemon juice and then mix in ½ tsp of the nori seaweed powder.

To assemble

Open up the bao buns and smear some chilli sauce on the bottom, followed by slices of cucumber and coleslaw.

Place the crab on next, followed by a small dollop of mayo and – if you like it hotter – another smear of chilli sauce on top.

Garnish and don't forget to squeeze the lime before eating.

 PAIR WITH

Sharp's Offshore Pilsner
Or any Pilsner or Pale Ale

MAIN
BEEF FEATHER BLADE WITH HERB OLIVE RELISH AND MISO SAUCE

SERVES 6

Sharp's Wolf Rock goes brilliantly with a piece of grilled steak. In this recipe the herb olive relish picks up on the herby hops, while the miso mimics the malty flavours. It's a great dish for a BBQ party.

For the beef

1 whole beef feather blade (approx. 2-2.5kg), trimmed and filleted

1 tsp chopped thyme

2 cloves garlic, crushed

1 tbsp rosemary, chopped

1 tbsp oregano, chopped

100ml olive oil

For the herb olive relish

100g flat parsley, chopped

50g basil, chopped

50g mint, chopped

4 spring onions, chopped

2 tbsp capers, chopped

6 salted anchovies, chopped

4 cloves garlic, crushed

100g mixed olives, chopped

2 lemons, juice

100ml extra virgin olive oil

Salt and pepper for seasoning

For the miso sauce

225g white miso

200g sugar

115ml sake

115ml mirin

For the beef

Ask your butcher to take a whole feather blade, trim off any sinew and fillet through the middle to remove all gristle.

Cut into 4 large portions (approx. 250g each).

Marinate the steaks (overnight or for at least 2 hours) in the olive oil, garlic, thyme, rosemary and oregano.

Refrigerate until needed.

Make the herb olive relish by mixing all the ingredients together, and refrigerate until needed.

Make the miso sauce by putting all the ingredients in a pan and warming until the sugar has dissolved.

Sear off your feather blade steaks in a hot pan or on the BBQ and cook to your liking. If you have a meat probe, cook to 54C – feather blade is best rare to medium rare.

Rest the steak for 8 minutes, then slice thinly and lay on a plate.

Dress with the herb olive relish and a drizzle of miso sauce.

Garnish with any bitter leaves such as watercress, rocket or mizuna and your favourite dressing.

 PAIR WITH

Sharp's Wolf Rock
Or an Amber Ale or a
traditional IPA

DESSERT
CHOCOLATE SALT CARAMEL POTS WITH MALT ICE CREAM

I love the chocolate malt flavours coming through and underlining the flavours of this dessert with a hit of salt caramel.

MAKES 4 POTS

For the ice cream
8 egg yolks

250g sugar

500ml milk

1ltr double cream

1 vanilla pod

60g Ovaltine (add more if you would like it more malty)

For the chocolate pot mix
250ml double cream

40g muscovado sugar

½ vanilla pod, split

1 egg

100g 70% dark chocolate chips

For the salt caramel
125g caster sugar

2 tbsp water

300ml double cream

3 egg yolks

Cornish sea salt to taste

PAIR WITH

Titanic Plum Porter
Or a Trappist Dubbel

For the ice cream

Whisk the egg yolks and sugar in a mixer until it triples in volume and is fluffy.

Heat the cream and milk together with a split vanilla pod and bring to the boil.

Mix the hot liquid into the egg and sugar mix, add the Ovaltine and stir over a low heat. Using a thermometer, you want to continue to stir the ice cream mix until it reaches 83C.

Cool down to fridge temperature and churn in an ice cream machine (using manufacturer's directions).

For the chocolate pot mix

Combine the cream, muscovado sugar and vanilla pod in a saucepan and bring to the boil.

Take off the heat, rain in the chocolate and whisk in the egg.

Divide the mix between 4 dessert glasses and set in the fridge.

For the salt caramel

Put the sugar and water in a saucepan and make a dark caramel.

Whisk in the double cream, making sure there are no lumps by heating and stirring.

Whisk in the yolks and season with sea salt.

Cool to room temperature and pour on top of the chocolate pot mix, then chill until needed.

When ready, pull out of the fridge and serve with a scoop of the malt ice cream. To be extra naughty, serve with clotted cream too.

DINNER PARTY TWO

BY ALYN WILLIAMS

STARTER
GRILLED WATERMELON WITH IBERICO HAM

This is a lovely, fresh, summery dish with lots of harmonious flavours.

SERVES 6

1 watermelon, ripe

18 slices good Iberico ham

1 English cucumber

Cucumber or courgette flowers

Salt

50g flat leaf parsley

1 lemon, zest and juice

1½ peaches

20 mint leaves

2 tsp chopped fennel tops

2 tbsp chopped chervil

75ml olive oil

PAIR WITH

Sierra Nevada Pale Ale
Or a New England IPA
or a Kölsch-style Beer

Pick the parsley leaves and blanch for 30 seconds in boiling water. Remove with a slotted spoon and refresh in iced water.

Squeeze out and return the parsley to the boiling water, then continue to cook until soft. Strain the leaves and blitz in a liquidiser until smooth, adding a little water if necessary to keep the puree moving around the blade.

Put the puree into a bowl over another bowl of ice, to cool down quickly.

Once cold, stir in the grated lemon zest, fennel, chervil and mint, followed by the oil and – lastly – enough lemon to give a nice acidity, and a good pinch of salt.

Peel the watermelon and slice into 2cm-thick slices. Heat a non-stick frying pan until very hot, smear a little oil on the melon slices, and cook in the pan until caramelised.

Remove from the pan and cut into 2cm dices, avoiding any clusters of seeds.

Quarter and de-stone the peaches, remove the skin carefully and cut each quarter in half.

Cut the cucumber in half lengthways and then in half again. Cut each strip on an angle into 1.5cm triangles.

Wash and cut the courgette flowers into thick strips.

To serve, smear the dressing on the base of a plate, dress the ingredients attractively, and sprinkle with a little Maldon salt just before serving.

ROASTED COD WITH FENNEL COMPOTE AND MAURITIAN CURRY SAUCE

This dish was inspired by a trip to Mauritius a couple of years ago. It has been a regular on the menu at The Westbury ever since.

SERVES 6

1 large fillet of cod, skin on, cut into 150g pieces

1 litre cold water

100g table salt

Olive oil

3 bulbs fennel

50g caster sugar

100ml white wine vinegar

2 pink grapefruits

12 fennel fronds

For the curry sauce

10g mild green chilli

10g medium red chilli

¼ hot red chilli

20g fresh coconut

4g tamarind paste

40g fried onion

4g fresh ginger

4g garlic

1g curry leaves

10g cashew nuts

1g fresh turmeric

1g coriander leaf

Boil the salt and water together to make a brine. Cool to fridge temperature.

Make sure the cod fillets have no bones in them, place into the cold brine and soak for 10 minutes, then wash well in cold water and pat dry.

Grate the fennel on a medium grater.

Heat the sugar and vinegar together until boiling rapidly. Stir in the grated fennel and cook for 8-10 minutes until tender.

Remove from the pan and pop into a dish to cool.

Peel the grapefruit and cut out the segments, cut each segment in half widthways and reserve.

Warm the cashews under the grill for a few seconds and slice very finely with a mandolin, reserve in a dry place.

Grind all of the curry sauce ingredients together into a paste (except the stock and cream), either using a pestle and mortar or a food processor.

Boil the fish stock and cream together and whisk in the curry paste to taste, seasoning with a little salt and a squeeze of lime juice if needed.

Roast the brined cod in a hot pan with a little olive oil on the skin until golden brown, then place a small sheet of parchment paper under the fish and cook in the oven, preheated to 170C, for 6-8 minutes.

RECIPE CONTINUED OVERLEAF...

MAIN
ROASTED COD WITH FENNEL COMPOTE AND MAURITIAN CURRY SAUCE

¼ g ground cumin

¼ g toasted coriander seeds

1g fenugreek seeds

6g muscovado sugar

6g shrimp paste

2g rock salt

500ml fish stock

200ml double cream

Maldon salt

To Garnish

16 cashew nuts

1 piece fresh coconut

Fresh lime, to taste

PAIR WITH

Hoegaarden
Or a German Wheat Beer,
or a Belgian Abbey Beer

Remove the fish carefully, season the skin with a pinch of Maldon salt and allow to rest while getting the other ingredients plated.

Using 2 spoons, make a large quenelle with the fennel compote, arrange the grapefruit segments and fennel fronds.

Arrange the fish on the plate and micro-plane the fresh coconut over it, followed by the sliced cashew nuts.

Pour the hot curry sauce around the fish and enjoy!

DESSERT
YOGHURT PANNA COTTA WITH RASPBERRIES AND FROZEN RICOTTA

This fresh and vibrant dessert is prepared in advance, ready to pull out as a lovely conclusion to a dinner party.

SERVES 6

500g Greek style yoghurt

150g whipping cream

2 leaves gelatine
(soaked in ice cold water)

50g icing sugar

100g raspberries for crushing

80 raspberries for garnish

1 lime, juice

100g ricotta (Sairas if available)

1 lemon, zest

10g icing sugar

1 Amalfi lemon (or a nice
unwaxed lemon if Amalfi
is not available)

PAIR WITH

Timmermans Framboise
Or a Trappist Tripel Ale
or a Raspberry Stout

Get 6 cocktail glasses or other stylish glasses.

Crush the raspberries with a fork until broken down but not pureed, then stir in a squeeze of lime juice.

Spoon the crushed raspberries into the bottom of the serving glasses.

Mix the yoghurt in a bowl until smooth, whisk the cream to soft peaks with the icing sugar and fold into the yoghurt.

Squeeze the water out of the gelatine and melt over a medium heat using a little milk. Once melted, cool a little, then beat into the yoghurt mixture using a rubber spatula.

Spoon the yoghurt mix over the crushed raspberries to cover, leaving room for the raspberries on top. Place the glasses in the fridge to set (which should take about an hour).

Beat the lemon zest and icing sugar into the ricotta, wrap into a cylinder with parchment paper and freeze overnight.

To serve, dress the raspberries with a squeeze of Amalfi lemon juice and pile them on top of the set yoghurt glasses. Using a micro-plane or extra-fine grater, generously grate the frozen ricotta over the top and finish with micro-planed Amalfi lemon zest.

Suggestion

If you prefer not to use gelatine you can find plant-based alternatives such as iota carrageenan, or simply don't set the yoghurt.

SHOWSTOPPER CHOCOLATE MOUSSE PYRAMID

This recipe has been a favourite of mine for a long time. It's easy to make, tastes delicious and looks amazing.

SERVES 8

For the sponge
12 eggs
375g sugar
275g flour
100g cocoa powder

For the ganache
240g double cream
480g dark chocolate

For the chocolate mousse
350g double cream
300g ganache

For the garnish
200g white chocolate
200g milk chocolate
Golden decoration spray

PAIR WITH

Guinness Milk Stout, or try another Stout, Porter or Barley Wine

BY STUART PATE

Whisk the eggs and sugar together to ribbon consistency (so when you hold the whisk over the mixture, the batter forms a ribbon that will hold its shape on the surface of the mixture).

Sieve the cocoa powder and flour together, then fold the dry ingredients into the eggs and sugar mix.

Pour into a 12-inch round cake tin and bake at 180C for 6-8 minutes.

When cooked, let it cool then cut into slices. From these slices cut out circles, decreasing in size so you can build a pyramid (you can get two circles out of one slice).

To make the ganache, heat the cream, then mix in the dark chocolate. Allow to cool to 38C.

Then make the chocolate mousse: whisk the cream to nearly ribbon consistency, add the melted (cooled) ganache and fold together.

Stack the cooled circles onto each other with chocolate mousse between each layer.

Once you have built a pyramid, coat the outside with the remaining mousse.

For the garnish, melt the white and milk chocolate and spread thinly onto plastic film (the sort of plastic that florists wrap flowers in), then leave to set.

Once set, break the chocolate into shards and stick onto the side of the pyramid.

Decorate with golden decoration spray to finish.

WINTER
WARMERS

On a cold winter's evening nothing beats hunkering down by the fire with great company, a hearty dish to warm your cockles, and a full-bodied beer to match.

SLOW COOKED PORK CHEEK, CHORIZO AND BUTTERBEAN CHILLI

A simple yet tender, delicious and warming dish that has become a firm winter favourite with our customers. In Cornwall we use the wonderful Primrose Herd for all our pork – use the best you can get your hands on for this dish.

SERVES 4

4-6 pork cheeks

350g top quality pork mince

300g cured or fresh chorizo sausage, sliced

400g kidney beans

400g butterbeans

400g passata or chopped tomatoes

1 large white onion, sliced

1-2 fresh chillies, diced

2 cloves garlic, crushed

10 cherry tomatoes

Knob of butter

2 tsp cumin seeds

2 tsp fennel seeds

2 tsp smoked paprika

1 tsp smoked chipotle paste

300g basmati rice

2 tsp turmeric

Soured cream, a dollop to serve

150g cheddar, grated

2 spring onions, sliced

PAIR WITH

Worthington White Shield
Or a traditional IPA or a Smoked Beer

BY NICK ARCHER

Melt the butter in a large pan on a medium heat, then brown off the pork cheeks and minced pork.

When nicely coloured add in the sliced chorizo, chilli, onions, crushed garlic, cherry tomatoes, cumin seeds, fennel seeds and chipotle paste. Keep the heat up and stir regularly until the onions have softened.

Add the kidney beans and butterbeans (and their water if using tinned), along with the passata, smoked paprika, salt and pepper. Mix it all well and bring to the boil before reducing to a gentle/low heat and placing a lid on, but not covering fully.

Simmer low and slow for a minimum of 4 hours, or until you are happy with how tender the pork cheeks are and how rich the sauce looks. We simmer ours for at least 8-10 hours! Stir every now and then, and add boiling water if needed to keep it loose.

Once the chilli is to your satisfaction, add the rice to a pan along with the turmeric and cook as per the packet instructions.

Plate up the rice and top generously with the chilli, ensuring each dish gets a pork cheek.

Top with a spoonful of soured cream, a sprinkling of cheddar and some of the sliced spring onions. Enjoy!

FISH PIE

Everyone has a go-to fish pie recipe. Mine has evolved over 20 years of running the kitchen at The Ivy. My family love it when I make a big dish for us all to share.

SERVES 4

1 small onion, finely diced

80g butter

40g plain flour

100ml white wine

200ml fish stock

1 tsp English mustard

60ml double cream

150g white fish fillet (such as cod, haddock, hake or pollock), skinned and diced

100g salmon fillet, skinned and diced

100g naturally smoked haddock fillet, skinned and diced

15g flat leaf parsley, finely chopped

800-900g large mashing potatoes, peeled and quartered

1 tbsp fresh white bread crumbs

1 tbsp freshly grated parmesan

Seasoning

PAIR WITH

Staropramen
Or a Light Pale Ale
or a Kölsch-style Beer

BY ALAN BIRD

Put the potatoes in a pan, cover with water, add a pinch of salt and bring to the boil.

While the potatoes are cooking, get on with making the sauce.

Gently cook the onion in 40g of the butter until soft, then stir in the flour and mix well.

Gradually whisk or stir in the white wine and fish stock, bring to the boil and season lightly with salt and pepper.

Simmer gently for 15 minutes, giving it an occasional stir, until it has reduced and thickened slightly.

Add the double cream, stir and simmer for another 5 minutes.

Add the chopped parsley and simmer for 2 minutes, remove from the heat and stir in the English mustard. If necessary, season again with salt and pepper to taste.

Leave the sauce to cool slightly before you begin building the pies – either into 4 individual ovenproof dishes or 1 large one.

Drain the boiled potatoes (making sure they are tender) and mash with the remaining butter and some seasoning. Leave to cool whilst building the pies.

Place a spoonful of sauce in the bottom of the dish, then add a layer of fish, then add a little more sauce and so on. Seasoning each layer as you go until the dish is filled almost to the top – leaving room for the mashed potato.

Using a piping bag or a fork, cover the fish pie mixture with the mashed potato (you will find it easier if it's still warm), then scatter with the breadcrumbs and parmesan.

Bake in an oven preheated to 190C for 30-40 minutes, until browned on top.

Serve with buttered green beans or peas.

EXMOOR BEEF AND SMOKED POTATO PIE

SERVES 4

This dish is a play on traditional beef pie, using flavoursome cuts sourced locally from Exmoor. The smoked potato works well with the rich cheek and oxtail.

BY DEZ TURLAND

For the smoked potato pie

300g ox cheek

300g oxtail

750ml Wolf Rock IPA

325ml veal jus (you should be able buy this ready made from the supermarket, but if not you can use a good quality beef stock)

100g carrots, chopped

100g onions, chopped

100g celery, chopped

1 sprig of thyme

2 bay leaves

400g King Edward potatoes

1 large King Edward potato (for lining the pastry ring)

50g butter

100ml milk

50ml double cream

100g carrots

2 shallots

1 clove black garlic

5g smoked sea salt

For the beef

600g beef blade

100g black treacle

1 sprig of thyme

400g king oyster mushrooms

50g butter

100ml double cream

To garnish (optional)

Truffle, grated

Nasturtium flowers

Mushroom powder

For the smoked potato pie

Seal the cheek and oxtail in a hot pan, then add the roughly chopped vegetables and herbs. Add the ale and jus, cover with a lid and cook for 4 hours at 140C, until tender.

When cool, pick the oxtail from the bone and pull apart the cheek. Reserve the cooking liquor for later.

Finely dice and sauté the carrot, shallot and black garlic, then add the cooled oxtail and cheek, and a little of the reserved cooking liquor. The remainder can be reduced and passed through a fine sieve for finishing the dish.

Peel and boil the potatoes until soft, drain and then smoke for 5 minutes (either in a smoker or wrapped in tin foil on a wire rack over woodchips in a deep tray). Mash with warm milk and cream, and finish with butter and smoked sea salt.

Line a 4cm pastry ring with thinly sliced potato and bake until crispy. Fill with pie mix and top with smoked mash.

For the beef and mushrooms

If you've got some high-tech cheffing equipment, vac pac the beef blade with the black treacle and thyme and cook for 75 minutes at 57C in a water bath. Or, you can baste the beef blade in the black treacle, place the thyme on top, cover and cook low and slow for 4 hours at 75C.

When ready, seal in a hot pan to caramelise.

Trim and reserve 8 halves of mushrooms.

Roughly cut and sauté the rest in butter until soft.

Add cream, bring to the boil, blitz and pass for puree.

When required, sauté the half mushrooms in butter until browned.

To serve

Dish up the potato pie with the beef and mushrooms, and garnish with grated truffle, nasturtium and mushroom powder (optional).

 PAIR WITH

Sharp's Wolf Rock
Or a Best Bitter or Red IPA

DEZ TURLAND

**PR & MARKETING CHEF
BREND HOTELS**

Seasonal food and good quality beer have always made the perfect match for Dez Turland.

A beer lover and foodie who cut his teeth in the kitchen of Michael Quinn MBE, Dez Turland has always enjoyed finding the perfect beer to pair with his dishes. "I think there's a natural affinity between beer and food. It's simply about finding the right balance between the two," he says.

Fortunate to have so many great breweries producing excellent quality beers in the South West, Dez teamed up with Sharp's at the Trencherman's Awards in 2016, where he created a main course to be served with his favourite beer, Sharp's Wolf Rock. It was such a success that it's included in the book on p162. "It's not about having a pint of beer. You can have a little taster to go with each course," he explains.

Working closely with local farmers, fishermen and producers, and promoting the importance of seasonality in his modern, British cooking, Dez believes the South West is home to the finest natural larder in the UK. And despite supermarkets still misleading consumers with a year-round supply of global produce, he has faith that the public are becoming more in tune with the seasons and more savvy about their food choices.

Far from The Ritz and Piccadilly where his cooking skills developed under megastar Michael Quinn, Dez has combined a successful career with a much more casual coastal and country lifestyle on the edge of Exmoor. "In this beautiful part of the world, people are more relaxed than in cities, so they have more time to enjoy their food – and even take it more seriously," he says. Now in his role as Marketing and PR Chef overseeing 11 hotels and 75 chefs, he's a man on a mission to put the South West in the spotlight as a truly awesome culinary destination – and to include beer and food matching in that spotlight.

SMOKED CHICKEN AND SWEETCORN RISOTTO

The bold smokiness of the chicken really works well in this classic rice dish. It's a recipe I cook at home for the whole family.

SERVES 6

1 whole smoked chicken
(approx. 700g)

1½ litres chicken stock

500g carnaroli risotto rice

100g onion, thinly diced

2 cloves garlic, micro-planed

150g unsalted butter

1 pinch thyme, chopped

10g tarragon, chopped

10g chervil, chopped

10g chives, chopped

100g sweetcorn

2 tbsp mascarpone

150g parmesan, grated

5 spring onions, sliced thinly

Lemon juice

PAIR WITH

Thornbridge Jaipur
Or a New World IPA or Milk Stout

BY JOHN WALTON

Take the skin off the chicken and keep to one side. Then take all the meat off the bone and keep the carcass to one side with the skin.

Infuse the skin and carcass in the chicken stock for a couple of hours, so you get a nice smokiness into the stock.

Dice the chicken into 1cm cubes and set to one side.

Put the butter in a large pan and slowly melt, then add the onions, garlic and thyme and cook until soft but not coloured.

Add the rice and mix well through the butter and onions.

Gradually add the infused stock a ladle at a time, cooking the rice until soft and tender.

Take off the heat and add the mascarpone and then the parmesan, and melt through.

Add the diced chicken, sweetcorn and spring onions then fold through well.

Finish the risotto with the chopped herbs and a little lemon juice to taste.

Add some shaved parmesan at the table.

SWEET POTATO, CAULIFLOWER AND COCONUT CURRY

A home staple; quick, easy and ever so moreish.

SERVES 4

1 tbsp vegetable oil

1 onion, cut into wedges

1 red onion, cut into wedges

1 small green chilli,
de-seeded and chopped

1 clove garlic, crushed

4 kaffir lime leaves,
deveined and finely chopped

1 small cauliflower, cut into florets

225g sweet potato, diced

1 packet baby sweetcorn,
cut in half lengthwise

1 packet bok choy,
cut into quarters lengthwise

200ml coconut milk

200ml vegan vegetable stock

½ tsp harissa (more if you like a hot curry)

Thai fragrant rice

25g coriander, roughly chopped

2 tbsp desiccated coconut

2 tbsp green pistachio nuts,
roughly chopped

BY KEN SYMONS

Heat the oil in a large saucepan and fry the onion wedges, chilli, garlic and kaffir lime leaves for 1-2 minutes, stirring occasionally.

Add the potatoes and cauliflower and cook for a further 5 minutes.

Stir in the coconut milk, stock and harissa, reduce the heat and cook until the potatoes are tender.

Add the baby sweetcorn and bok choy, and cook for a further 2 minutes.

Cook the rice according to instructions.

In a dry frying pan, add the desiccated coconut and stir until golden, then add the chopped pistachio nuts and cooked rice, and gently mix together.

Place into four individual serving bowls and sprinkle with coriander.

Serve with your curry. Enjoy.

 PAIR WITH

Vedett White
Or a Belgian Witbier
or German Weisse

BREAD AND BUTTER PUDDING

This dish is a true classic that people love. It reminds me of my time spent working with Gary Rhodes.

SERVES 4-6

12 slices of white bread

250g butter

30g sultanas, soaked in a high ABV Belgian Dubbel or Barley Wine for at least a week

450ml double cream

150ml milk

2 vanilla pods

140g egg yolk

175g caster sugar

PAIR WITH

Innis & Gunn Original Or a Barrel-aged Beer or a Barley Wine

BY PAUL AINSWORTH

Place the butter in a pan and bring to the boil, whisking all the time until it turns nut brown. Then pass through a fine sieve, whisk until cool and leave to set at room temperature.

For the custard, whisk the eggs and the sugar together until pale and light.

Bring the cream, milk and vanilla to the boil, then pour over the egg and sugar mixture, whisking all the time.

Bring a pan with water to the simmer, then place the custard mixture in the bowl over the water and cook out until thick – stirring all the time.

Once the custard is thick and about 75-80C, pass through a fine sieve and leave to cool to room temperature.

Now butter your bread with the caramelised butter, cut off all the crusts from the bread and cut each slice into 4 triangles.

Lightly butter a small Pyrex dish and sprinkle some soaked sultanas on the base of the dish.

Dip the buttered bread triangles into the custard and lay into the dish, forming a single layer of bread with no gaps, then sprinkle some more sultanas on top of the bread.

Ladle a small amount of custard over this layer, then repeat this bread layer twice more.

On the third and final bread layer don't put any sultanas on top, just cover with the remaining custard.

Place cling film on top and leave at room temperature for at least 12 hours (making this the day before is fine). This helps the custard to really soak into the layers.

Place the dish inside a deep oven tray and fill the tray with warm water to the height of the bread and butter.

Place into a preheated oven at 110C and cook for 1 hour, until the custard is nice and thick. You can leave the cling film on top when baking as this will stop the top from drying in the oven.

To finish and give the bread and butter pudding an amazing texture, sprinkle caster sugar on top and blow torch to caramelise like a crème brûlée.

Serve with vanilla ice cream for a real treat.

SPICED CHOCOLATE FONDANT

This recipe originates from my days at The Ivy, when Phil Usher (my head pastry chef back then) and I, would bounce ideas off each other and try out different recipes. You can experiment too, by using your favourite liqueur in place of the Drambuie.

MAKES 12 PORTIONS

For the filling

70g dark chocolate (buttons or small pieces)

50ml double cream

20ml Drambuie

50g mincemeat

For the fondant

300g butter, unsalted

300g white chocolate (buttons or small pieces)

10g baking powder

5g mixed spice

3g ground cinnamon

260g flour

5 eggs, separated

90g caster sugar

200g currants and sultanas, soaked in hot water

PAIR WITH

La Trappe Dubbel, or a Barley Wine

BY ALAN BIRD

For the filling

Bring the cream to the boil, remove from the heat and stir in the chocolate until melted.

Stir in the Drambuie and mincemeat and leave to set in the fridge.

When set, mould into 25g balls.

For the fondant

Line the inside of 6/7cm stainless steel cooking rings with silicone paper. Cut squares of silicone paper and place them under each of the rings, and place on a baking sheet 6-7cm apart.

Preheat the oven to 190C.

Melt the butter and white chocolate in a bowl over a pan of simmering water. Don't let it get too hot. Meanwhile, sieve together the baking powder, spices and flour.

Mix the egg yolks into the chocolate (at this stage it may look like it's split, but it will come back when the flour is added) and then gently fold in the sieved flour mixture.

Whisk the egg whites and sugar until stiff, then whisk ¼ of this into the chocolate. When mixed, fold the rest of the egg whites in and then the currants and sultanas.

Half fill the moulds then add a ball of the filling and top up with the rest of the mixture.

Bake the fondants for 12 minutes.

Remove from the oven and loosen with a knife, then carefully put onto warmed serving plates with a spatula.

Serve with pouring cream or clotted cream - or just as they are.

Item: Tom Relish
Use By:
Date: 14/5
Shelf Life:
Emp: Mgr:
Qty:
Slow's Slack
Place label here

LARDER & CHEESE

Take time to cook up some treats for your larder and you'll be reaping the benefits for weeks. Cheese and chutney make a classic match for beer and you'll find some great flavour matching opportunities.

PLUM CHUTNEY

BY HENK DE VILLIERS FERREIRA

This chutney is a little bit sour and goes perfectly with my Pork Rillette (p38) as it counter balances the richness of it.

MAKES 1 JAR

500g ripe plums
2 shallots, finely chopped
125ml cider vinegar
100g caster sugar
Salt and pepper

Stone the plums and roast in an oven at 180C for 25 minutes. This will intensify the flavour and colour.

Sauté the shallots and add the other ingredients. Then cook on a low heat for 30 minutes until all the plums have broken down.

Allow to cool and refrigerate. You can keep this in the fridge for about a month.

DOOM BAR AND PEAR CHUTNEY

BY ZACK HAWKE

Great for grazing platters with cured meats, cheeses, bread and pickles.

MAKES 1 KILNER JAR

500g pears, peeled, cored and diced
150g brown sugar
250ml Sharp's Doom Bar
100ml cider vinegar
1 onion, diced
50g raisins
1 stick celery, peeled and diced
1 tsp ginger, grated
1 clove garlic, pasted
½ tsp cayenne
2 tsp salt
½ tsp cinnamon
½ tsp cloves
2 tsp mustard seeds

Put all ingredients in a large saucepan, and cook on low for 2 hours until thick and syrupy.

This will keep for up to 3 months in a sterilised jar.

TOMATO RELISH

BY ZACK HAWKE

The perfect partner for sardines, burgers, grilled mackerel, or cold meats and sandwiches.

MAKES 1 KILNER JAR

2kg ripe tomatoes, chopped

2 white onions, peeled and diced

200g caster sugar

150ml malt vinegar

2 pinches Cornish sea salt

1 tsp paprika

2 cloves

2 star anise

In a large saucepan, sweat the onions until soft but not coloured.

Add the chopped tomatoes, malt vinegar, salt, cloves, star anise and cook for 1 hour on low heat, stirring occasionally. The tomatoes should be a soft pulp.

Add the sugar and stir, then cook for a further 30 minutes.

Pass the sauce through a sieve and if needed return to the pan, increase the heat and reduce until the sauce has a thick consistency.

This can keep for up to 6 months in sterilised jars.

DOOM BAR PICKLED MUSSELS

BY ZACK HAWKE

Pickled mussels and shellfish are an old seaside tradition and this is our beer-fuelled take on them. If you're not a fan of shellfish, you can pickle vegetables instead using this pickling liquor.

MAKES 1 KILNER JAR

100ml Doom Bar, plus 100ml extra to steam the mussels open

100ml water

100ml demerara sugar

100ml malt vinegar

1kg Porthilly mussels, cleaned and de-bearded

In a saucepan combine the Doom Bar, sugar, vinegar and water, then boil until the sugar has dissolved.

Cool the pickling liquor down.

Heat a saucepan with a lid on until it is very hot, throw in your mussels and add your cooking Doom Bar.

Put the lid on immediately and let cook for 2 minutes, then stir the mussels and check they are all open.

Strain your mussels through a colander, pick the meat out of the shells onto a tray and chill them in the fridge until cold.

Mix the mussels and the pickling liquor and keep in a sterilised mason jar for up to 5 days.

Serve in a bowl with cocktail sticks.

BEER & CHEESE

A great way to start your own voyage of discovery in beer and food matching, beer and cheese pairing is fun and easy. Plus, when you find the right pairing it can be quite magical. Why not go to your local deli or supermarket, grab a selection of cheese and a selection of beers, and find out what works for you?

CHEESE STYLE	SUGGESTED BEER STYLE
Goat's cheese	Belgian Tripel
Stilton/Blue cheese	Barley Wine
Cheddar	Amber Ale/Best Bitter
Brie/Camembert	Pale Ale/IPA
Smoked cheese	Stout/Porter/Smoked (Rauch) Beer
Fruit cheese	Strong Red Ale
Soft mild cheese (Mozarella/Ricotta/Burrata)	Lager/Pilsner
Feta	Stout/Porter
Gouda/Gruyère/Emmental	IPA/Pale Ale

From rolling pastures to coastline,
Cornwall has inspired a new generation
of food and drink connoisseurs.

THE CHEFS

All the chefs in the book are close to our hearts and have ventured
with us on our food and beer journey. Not only are we fortunate to
have collaborated with such a talented bunch, we couldn't have got
to where we are in the process of beer and food pairing without the
support and knowledge of these expert foodies. Thank you.

PAUL AINSWORTH
PAUL AINSWORTH AT NO.6, PADSTOW

A name that rolls off the tongue as one of the most famous chefs in Cornwall, Paul is the talent behind two of Padstow's most applauded eateries – Paul Ainsworth at No.6 and Rojano's in the Square. Southampton born, he made his way to Cornwall via the kitchens of Gary Rhodes, Gordon Ramsay and Marcus Wareing. In 2011 he trumped some of the nation's top chefs when he made it to the final of BBC2's Great British Menu, and he was awarded his first Michelin star by 2012. Recognised for his unique style of cooking, Paul's dishes showcase the best Cornish produce sourced from local farmers, fishermen and artisan suppliers.

paul-ainsworth.co.uk/number6

TIM BARNES
OUTLAW'S FISH KITCHEN, PORT ISAAC

The Head Chef of Outlaw's Fish Kitchen spent childhood holidays in Cornwall, so it was natural to relocate to the coast in 2010, where he started out as KP in Nathan Outlaw's Seafood and Grill. It wasn't long until he moved into fine dining, after which Nathan packed him off to college and put him in charge of the kitchen within five years. Working with the freshest Cornish fish from Newlyn, along with seasonal veg from local suppliers, encourages Tim to keep his food simple and let the ingredients be the star of the show. Just like with wine and food, Tim uses the distinct flavours of different beers to match with seafood and other dishes.

nathan-outlaw.com/outlaws-fish-kitchen

NICK ARCHER
THE SHELLFISH PIG, MOBILE STREET FOOD

Husband and wife team Nick and Nikki Archer moved to Cornwall almost a decade ago, so that Nick could pursue a Marine Science degree. Blown away by Cornwall's lifestyle and landscapes, Nick turned back to his cheffing and travelling roots to set up an award-winning mobile food van, serving up produce from the coastline the pair are so passionate about. Having already forged relationships with fishermen and suppliers through Nick's studies, the couple focussed on seafood dishes and sustainability. Having worked on the Secret Bar with the Sharp's team, Nick has embraced the delights of beer and food matching, and loves sharing his passion and knowledge with his customers.

theshellfishpig.co.uk

ALAN BIRD
ALAN BIRD FOOD ETC, LONDON & HERTS

Lured to Cornwall by childhood memories of Cornish pasties, saffron buns, crab sandwiches and Cornish ice cream, Alan is a huge ambassador of the county's wealth of wonderful ingredients. Having worked at The Ivy restaurant and been personal chef to Lord Andrew Lloyd Webber, it's only natural that he ended up running his own business catering for VIP clients (Alan Bird Food Etc Ltd). Long-time friends with The Seafood Restaurant's Stephane Delourme, Alan also worked on the opening of Trevisker's Kitchen with Henk De Villiers Ferreira. Having created dishes for Sharp's Secret Bar pop-up, Alan believes that good beer can challenge the best of wines.

@ChefBird

STEPHANE DELOURME
THE SEAFOOD RESTAURANT, PADSTOW

Hailing from Quiberon in Brittany, Stephane has always had a penchant for the coast and grew up eating Fruits de Mer instead of Sunday roast. Working in Dublin, Paris and London, he always focussed his cooking around fish and shellfish, honing the skills that led him to become Head Chef at Stein's Seafood Restaurant – a position he has held for over 20 years. His relationship with Sharp's has blossomed since they worked together to develop Chalky's Bite in 2006, and since then matching beer with food is a natural part of the dining scene at Stein's. Stephane believes that beer drinking is in the British DNA and the right beers pair wonderfully with seafood.

rickstein.com/eat-with-us/the-seafood-restaurant

ROSS GEACH
PADSTOW KITCHEN GARDEN, PADSTOW

Nearly 20 years after leaving the same school as Ed Hughes, Ross is proud to be drinking Sharp's beer and cooking at his family farm in Padstow. What started out as a hobby for the sixth generation farmer has grown into a booming business – the former Stein's Head Chef turned Head Grower at Padstow Kitchen Garden now supplies vegetables and salad to some of the finest restaurants in Cornwall and beyond. Ross didn't consider matching fine dining with beer until Ed introduced him to the concept a few years ago, and he now understands how the delicate and complex flavours of beer can play an important part in any menu.

padstowkitchengarden.co.uk

HENK DE VILLIERS FERREIRA
TREVISKER'S, PADSTOW

South African-born Henk is somewhat famous in Cornwall for his mouth-watering steaks and meat. Inheriting his passion and knowledge about beef from his cattle farming grandfather, his expertise in butchery and the science of beef ageing enables him to serve up some of the most succulent cuts in the West Country. Having developed a loyal following during his five years helming the kitchen at Trevose Golf and Country Club, he has now opened his own Trevisker's Kitchen near Padstow. His mission is simple: to dish up fuss-free, quality food that echoes the coastal and country lifestyle of North Cornwall.

treviskers.com

ZACK HAWKE
THE MARINERS, ROCK

Having grown up in the surfing Mecca of Newquay, Zack trained under Nick Hodges at Lusty Glaze Beach, and has worked for Nathan Outlaw for over five years. Now Head Chef at The Mariners, he focuses on using the best ingredients and "doesn't mess around with them", because "Cornwall has the finest suppliers and produce in the country". Since he started at The Mariners, Zack has been working with Ed Hughes, experimenting with beer and food, and working with the complexities of both to come up with the perfect match.

nathan-outlaw.com/mariners-rock

JUDE KEREAMA
KOTA AND KOTA KAI, PORTHLEVEN

Hailing from New Zealand, Jude quit the London rat race to open Kota and Kota Kai in Cornwall. Bringing his Maori and Chinese-Malay roots into his cooking, Jude combines the best from land and sea in signature Asian-fused dishes. He can't help but let his style be influenced by the coastal lifestyle and his Rockpool dish (featured on the BBC's Great British Menu) is named after his favourite pastime with his son. Having teamed up with Sharp's for a few events, he is a huge fan of pairing beer and food, and can recommend a beer to go with all of his dishes.

kotarestaurant.co.uk

JAMES KNAPPET
AND SANDIA CHANG
BUBBLEDOGS AND KITCHEN TABLE, LONDON

Serving meticulously sourced Cornish ingredients in an exclusive dining venue in London, Sandia Chang and her partner, James Knappet, have long been ambassadors of Cornish produce and the Cornish lifestyle. James' early cheffing days were spent alongside Rick Stein at The Seafood Restaurant, and the pair are close friends with John Walton at Number 6. After a visit to Sharp's Secret Bar at the Padstow Christmas Festival, they quickly realised that beers can have same complexity as fine wines and can be perfectly matched with dishes in a Michelin Star restaurant such as theirs.

bubbledogs.co.uk

STEVE MARSH
CHEF CONSULTANT, PERRANPORTH

Steve's motto has always been to start with the best ingredients and let them speak for themselves. He moved to Cornwall over a decade ago, and believes that with the abundance of amazing seafood and vegetables available, there is no better place in the UK where all the ingredients come together so easily. His love for fine dining stemmed from working under Mark Raffan at the Gravetye, and he met Ed Hughes when Nathan Outlaw pipped him to the post for the Head Chef position at the St Enodoc Hotel. With a knack for pairing the earthy flavours of beers with different foods, he helped put a beer and food menu together with Henk at Trevisker's.

@Steve_Marshchef

CHRIS MCCLURG
PAUL AINSWORTH AT NO.6, PADSTOW

The Sous Chef at the prestigious Number 6, Chris was born and raised in Belfast. He started exploring his passion for all things food related at the tender age of 16, working in the kitchen with Brian McCann at Shu Restaurant. Arriving in Cornwall in 2011, via pit stops in London and Brussels, Chris is a key figure in the kitchen at Number 6 and a name to watch out for in the future.

paul-ainsworth.co.uk/number6

BEN PRIOR
BEN'S CORNISH KITCHEN, MARAZION

Following in his grandad's footsteps when he moved to Cornwall to open his own restaurant, Ben brings over 20 years of catering experience to his popular establishment in Marazion. Using as much local produce as possible to create a menu that echoes the seasons, Ben favours a clean, fresh style of cooking, reflecting the crisp, fresh feeling of the coastal air in Cornwall. Having been on board with Ed's passion for beer and food pairing for years, Ben believes that beer has as much complexity as wine, and is as much of a product of its origins and production as the food served.

benscornishkitchen.com

STUART PATE
RICK STEIN, PADSTOW

Stein's Head Patisserie Chef has always been drawn to the sea. He jumped at the chance to move down from London and help set up Stein's Patisserie in Padstow, a move back to his wife's roots in the West Country. Lured by the buzz of cheffing life in Padstow, whilst also having 'paradise' on the doorstep, Stuart is now mainly based at The Seafood Restaurant and Stein's Cookery School, while also working on new projects, cooking demos and Stein's apprenticeship scheme.

rickstein.com/eat-with-us/the-seafood-restaurant

TRISTAN STEPHENSON
AUTHOR AND BARTENDER

Tristan Stephenson is an award-winning bartender, barista and author. During a career spanning almost 20 years, he has opened eight bars and restaurants in London and Cornwall, travelled to over 300 distilleries around the world and published six books on the subject of alcohol, including the bestselling *The Curious Bartender: The Artistry & Alchemy of Creating the Perfect Cocktail*.

thecuriousbartender.com

KEN SYMONS
OLIVER'S, FALMOUTH

A proud Cornishman, Ken's cooking style draws on 50 years of working in Falmouth, and his fantastic friendships with the finest Cornish suppliers. His passion for working with local farmers and producers is reflected in the quality and diversity of the dishes served at his much-lauded restaurant, Oliver's, where tables are booked up months ahead. A key player in Cornwall's cheffing community, Ken is good friends with fellow chefs Ben Prior and Jude Kereama. Having met Ed Hughes at the Cornish Chef Club – an initiative bringing chefs and suppliers together – he is also an ambassador of the beer and food movement.

oliversfalmouth.com

JOHN WALTON
PAUL AINSWORTH AT NO.6, PADSTOW

Padstow born-and-bred, John is driven by a life-long passion for cooking local produce. Having met Paul Ainsworth in 2003 when they were both working under Marcus Wareing in London, Paul was keen to have John back by his side when he opened Number 6. Having been the Head Chef here since the early days, Paul holds John in high regard as not only a fantastic leader and mentor, but also as the glue that holds the team together.

paul-ainsworth.co.uk/number6

DEZ TURLAND
BREND HOTELS, NORTH DEVON

Arriving in Cornwall via the Ritz Hotel, Dez helped open the Alverton Manor in Truro, before helming the kitchens at Falmouth's Greenbank Hotel and The Royal Duchy. Now in North Devon overseeing more than 75 chefs for the Brend Hotel Group, he works closely with farmers, fishermen, producers and other chefs, to promote the South West as an awesome culinary destination. Bowled over by Ed Hughes' knowledge and enthusiasm for beer and food matching, Dez believes that pairing the right beer and food can lift a dish to new heights, whilst also showcasing the complex natures of a really great brew.

brend-hotels.co.uk

ALYN WILLIAMS
ALYN WILLIAMS AT THE WESTBURY, MAYFAIR AND THE WILD RABBIT, KINGHAM

Williams' culinary journey started at home where his father grew vegetables and cooked with a passion that was passed onto Alyn at a tender age. Alyn worked with some of the biggest names in the business, including Gordon Ramsay and Marcus Wareing, before opening his own restaurant, Alyn Williams at The Westbury. His light, progressive style of cooking won him the coveted 'National Chef of the Year' title in 2012, along with his first Michelin Star. He has also taken on the role of Chef Patron at The Wild Rabbit, located just a short walk from the market garden where Alyn handpicks the vegetables used on the menu.

alynwilliams.com

HOSPITALITY ACTION

Thank you for buying this book. £1 of the proceeds will be donated to Hospitality Action, a charity that supports people working in the hospitality industry.

Hospitality is a stressful industry, with long hours, high-pressure environments and physically demanding work. Behind the smiles and slick service, hospitality workers can fall upon hard times. Injuries, mental health problems and addiction are sadly a feature of modern life in the trade.

At Hospitality Action we offer workers financial, physical and psychological support to help them overcome adversity and get back to work as quickly as possible. We offer assistance to individuals and families, helping them stay afloat with grants to cover anything from rent payments to school uniform for their children. And for those who sadly can't return to the industry they love, we provide ongoing support in the transition to the next stage of their lives.

For older people who have retired from the industry, we offer grants to help with heating bills, home conversions or even funeral costs for loved ones. We also provides a lifeline to prevent loneliness and isolation, and our 'Golden Friends' enjoy regular contact and local events to help them stay active and connected to their community.

So thanks again for buying this cookery book. You've already made a difference to somebody in the hospitality industry.

To find out more about Hospitality Action and the difference we make visit www.hospitalityaction.org.uk

THE HOSPITALITY ACTION TEAM

USEFUL INFO

AUTHORS

Now you're ready to start cooking dishes to pair with beer, here's a quick conversion chart if you prefer using imperial measurements.

OVEN TEMPS

50C - 122F
60C - 140F
70C - 158F
80C - 176F
90C - 194F
100C - 212F
110C - 230F
120C - 248F
130C - 266F
140C - 284F
150C - 302F
160C - 320F
170C - 338F
180C - 356F
190C - 374F
200C - 392F

LIQUIDS

10ml - 0.35 fl oz
50ml - 1.75 fl oz
100ml - 3.5 fl oz
200ml - 7 fl oz
500ml - 17.5 fl oz
750ml - 26 fl oz
1ltr - 35 fl oz

WEIGHT

5g - 0.2oz
10g - 0.35oz
50g - 1.8oz
100g - 3.5oz
200g - 7oz
300g - 10.5oz
400g - 14.1oz
500g - 1lb 2oz
600g - 1lb 5oz
700g - 1lb 9oz
800g - 1lb 12oz
900g - 2lb
1000g - 2lb 3oz

ED HUGHES

Ed Hughes is a beer sommelier at Sharp's with a wealth of experience in the beer industry. His mission is to dispel the myths of beer drinking and bring beer to the dining table alongside the finest seasonal ingredients.

RACHEL WILLIAMS

Rachel Williams is Communications Manager at Sharp's where she has worked for over a decade, promoting the brewery's work in beer and food.

HAYLEY SPURWAY

Hayley Spurway is a writer, traveller and gastronome whose work is entrenched in the Cornish coastal lifestyle.

INDEX

ACKNOWLEDGEMENTS

ED HUGHES AND RACHEL WILLIAMS

Producing this book has been a dream of ours for a long time. And what an incredible experience it's been!

To mention everyone involved in our journey is an almost impossible task (so apologies to anyone we've missed) but we'd like to thank everyone below, without whom this book would never have happened.

THANKS TO...

All of the chefs involved, who have given us not only their beloved recipes, but also their valuable time. These people have inspired us with their generosity of spirit, expert knowledge of flavours and willingness to champion beer with food.

Paul Ripley, our first Secret Bar chef, who sadly couldn't be involved in the book but has been a huge part of our story.

Nathan Outlaw, for the forword and for being one of our heroes and main inspirations for the book.

Zack Hawke, for going above and beyond in the name of this book (and in general for Sharp's).

Photographer Guy Harrop, who has produced some beautiful shots and been a joy to work with.

Louise, Hayley and Steve at Muse Media for their expertise in publishing and guiding us on our maiden cookbook voyage.

Nick, Jo and the team at Salt Media for supporting our work in beer and food and introducing us to some of the awesome chefs in this book via the Trencherman's Awards events.

Molson Coors and Sharp's (especially Emma Roderick, James Nicholls, Martin Coyle and Jim Shearer) for their leadership and for believing in the project from the start.

The band of outlaws - Tom Brown, Ian Dodgson, Andrew Sawyer and Pete Biggs - who have shared kitchens, services and stages with us over the years and provided us with some incredible food along the way.

Carla at Mariners Lettings, Mr and Mrs Sellars, and Nicky Roads - for lending us their beautiful homes for the location shoots.

All the suppliers who provided fantastic ingredients for the tastiest, best-looking food we could ever ask for.

All of our friends and colleagues who took part in the photos for this book - for their enthusiasm, good humour and dashing good looks.

The brewers of the brilliant beers that have featured in the book (and those that haven't). The hard work and dedication it takes to brew consistently great beer should never be underestimated!

And finally, MASSIVE thanks to the whole Sharp's Brewery family, past, present and future, for their unending passion and dedication to beer.

We hope you have enjoyed this book and will continue your own beer and food journey!

FOLLOW US FOR MORE INSPIRATION